SELF–LEARNING MANA

Diversity, Equity, and Inclusion Essentials

You Always Wanted To Know

Cultivating organizational culture for competitive edge

DR. DENEAN ROBINSON

Diversity, Equity, and Inclusion Essentials You Always Wanted To Know

First Edition

Paperback ISBN 10: 1-63651-297-6
Paperback ISBN 13: 978-1-63651-297-6

Ebook ISBN 10: 1-63651-298-4
Ebook ISBN 13: 978-1-63651-298-3

Hardback ISBN 10: 1-63651-299-2
Hardback ISBN 13: 978-1-63651-299-0

Library of Congress Control Number: 2024946690

This publication is designed to provide accurate and authoritative information in regard to the subject matter covered. The Author has made every effort in the preparation of this book to ensure the accuracy of the information. However, information in this book is sold without warranty either expressed or implied. The Author or the Publisher will not be liable for any damages caused or alleged to be caused either directly or indirectly by this book.

Vibrant Publishers books are available at special quantity discount for sales promotions, or for use in corporate training programs. For more information please write to bulkorders@vibrantpublishers.com

Please email feedback / corrections (technical, grammatical or spelling) to spellerrors@vibrantpublishers.com

To access the complete catalogue of Vibrant Publishers, visit www.vibrantpublishers.com

About the Author

 **Dr. Denean Robinson** is an experienced higher education professor and human resource consultant. Over the past 19 years, she has developed and facilitated marketing, human resource development, organizational behavior, organizational development, change management, and strategic management courses/seminars at various universities and organizations across the Washington DC metropolitan area. Due to her industry knowledge in the human resources arena, she has been involved in conducting several customized training for various nationally known SHRM agencies for their participants' professional development retooling purposes.

She has authored open educational resource and human resource books for community colleges in Maryland and has significant experience in nonprofit management operating state social service agencies. Currently, Dr. Robinson operates as a staff development trainer consultant and is working on developing written content in the areas of emotional intelligence and employee engagement for executive leaders.

This page is intentionally left blank

What experts say about this book!

In an age where divisiveness seems to be the order of the day, we sorely need the lessons that Dr. Robinson teaches in her latest book. Organizations need the power of inclusiveness, achieved through equity and a celebration of diversity to be resilient enough, nimble enough, and innovative enough to succeed as world societies and economies continue to grow more intimately dependent on one another. As Drs. Hersey and Blanchard taught us how to be situational leaders, Dr. Robinson takes us further on the leadership journey and gives us all a path toward becoming distributed leaders so we can capitalize on a wider range of ideas, approaches, and outcomes for our organizations. Thank you, Dr. Robinson!

**– Toby R. Gouker, PhD, Graduate Program Director,
University of Maryland**

Dr. Denean Robinson has penned an insightful and thought-provoking book to help us to better understand, and appreciate, the tenets of diversity, equity, and inclusion. In this Self-Learning Management series, the ten chapters of *Diversity Equity Inclusion Essentials You Always Wanted to Know: Cultivating Organizational Culture for Competitive Advantage* capture important learning objectives that ultimately heighten our individual and collective awareness of the five key concepts that are highlighted at the end of the book. It is well-researched through multiple sources and contains a plethora of graphics for the benefit of visual learners. This is a must-buy and highly recommended!

**– Kevin Wayne Johnson, Founder & CEO,
The Johnson Leadership Group LLC.**

This book belongs in the library of any business manager. It is a clear exposition of the history and need for DEI initiatives in the modern business world. Dr. Robinson describes the moral imperatives for such a program (especially in the world of higher education) and also makes a strong business case for DEI efforts.

Diversity, Equity, and Inclusion Essentials You Always Wanted to Know is a book that fulfills many purposes. It is a manual about DEI for management and provides a blueprint for successfully implementing such a program. The author analyzes important concepts, including but not limited to the importance of corporate culture and how to transform it when implementing a DEI policy. It also describes how DEI initiatives can fit into an organization's strategic plan. I especially appreciated the discussion of metrics when measuring the effectiveness of a DEI program.

Aside from the many practical uses of this book, it is simply a very good read. Dr. Robinson writes clearly and in an easily digestible manner, unlike many books dealing with complex subjects. Even if you are not primarily responsible for DEI efforts in your organization, this book provides essential information about why DEI can benefit your organization and the economy as a whole. I highly recommend it.

– Mark Koscinski, CPA, D.Litt., Associate Professor of Accounting Practice, Moravian University

Diversity, Equity, and Inclusion Essentials You Always Wanted to Know by Dr. Denean Robinson is a practical guide for leaders aiming to integrate DEI principles into their organizations for long-term success. With over two decades of experience, Dr. Robinson highlights the essential role DEI plays in fostering innovation, resilience, and adaptability in a globalized market. The book addresses the complexities of DEI, offering strategies to navigate leadership divides and emphasizing the importance of cultural competence and empathy. Dr. Robinson argues that understanding and embracing diversity is crucial not only for creating inclusive workplaces but also for driving sustainable business growth, making this book a valuable resource for leaders and HR professionals.

– Professor Felicia Bowen, MBA, Associate Professor, Prince George's Community College

Table of Contents

Acknowledgments

This book would not have been possible without the loving support of my mother, Eleanor Robinson. She was my first teacher and my greatest inspiration in accomplishing all things possible by instructing me to keep God first and family close. To my best friend Anita Jones, encouraging me to strive to achieve success by always reaching for the stars no matter how far they seem.

In this world, you need to have professional mentors who provide you with words of wisdom and guide you through your journey of life. These mentors are Professor Felicia Bowen, Professor Denise-Bailey Gibson, Dr. Toby Gouker, Mr. Kevin Wayne Johnson, Ms. Gnansi Konan, and Dr. Charles Perry. I can't forget about my hair stylist, Ms. Travena Bunn. She makes sure I am always looking like a professional. Finally, to my students who provided me with a light to learn and a platform to inspire, motivate, and groom for professional success. "Educate to Delete the Hate" are the words I live by to change the negatives of the world into positive beginnings.

This page is intentionally left blank

Preface

Diversity, equity, and inclusion (DEI) is not only a framework, but a mindset that business leaders should embrace to better connect with customers and build strong partnerships across various social and economic groups. In the 21st century, businesses that tap into multicultural manufacturers and distributors will be able to expand their diversification portfolio. This will allow businesses to introduce their products to a multitude of individuals and geographical areas that have never been a part of their cultural framework. By reading this book, business leaders will be able to examine their organizational structure of creating a DEI strategy to increase their bottom line.

Part of the challenge for society and business leaders to accept DEI initiatives is the profound perception that this issue only represents black and white instead of an equilibrium of understanding and building new industry knowledge and creating a workplace atmosphere of critical thinking and synergy to both your internal and external customers. Without forecasting and creating sustainable changes within the organizational structure, an organization will suffer negative profitability consequences and negate its ability to connect with all stakeholders associated with its strategic lifeline.

This book will provide a theoretical and practical overview of how DEI will enhance an organization's ability to develop competitive advantage, create a sustainable and motivated work culture, and hire and build emotional intelligence leaders which will lead to a blueprint for a more transformational and innovative product.

This page is intentionally left blank

Introduction

As the 21st century revolutionizes itself and brushes off dealing with the effects of one of the most horrific health pandemics (COVID-19), it becomes clearer that unless organizations can adapt and be flexible in building their core competencies and workforce to face these ever-ending changes, they will no longer be able to be relevant in meeting the needs of the constituents or competitive in their prospective industry.

Diversity, equity, and inclusion (DEI) is the new storm that organizations must address in order to survive and thrive in reaching their maximum potential as a shaker and mover in their industry. DEI allows organizations to create policies and procedures and set ethical standards of maintaining and creating rigorous initiatives that allow their workforce to capture the essence of active participation in decision-making freedom.

Organizations that invest in DEI initiatives are more likely to develop a comprehensive product/service that will represent the melting pot of our society. DEI introduces the concepts of unification, accountability, and fair and equitable opportunity for everyone who is involved with the organization. The major components of DEI include concentrating on leadership development, creating SWOT goals, enhancing training opportunities for both internal and external stakeholders, and finally, developing organizational culture and policies that incorporate emotional intelligence practices.

The topic of diversity, equity, and inclusion is so controversial because of the misunderstanding of this initiative. This act was not to create a separation of men versus women, black versus white, or rich versus poor but to create an action that provides a framework for everyone to have an opportunity to stimulate creativity and innovation inside their prospective organization. DEI is a strategic guide or checklist that trains senior leaders in organizations to examine authenticity and how it can bring a sense of belonging and motivate their workforce in implementing solutions to prospective problems. DEI allows leaders to compete and create alternative products and services to meet the demands of their various customer backgrounds. By incorporating a DEI framework, policies, processes, training, recruitment, and engagement activities will begin to mirror the external market. This will ultimately lead organizations to have socio and economic leverage in sustaining competitive advantage in their industry market.

By the end of the book, you should be in a position to understand the following:

- The meaning of diversity, equity, and inclusion and their key components

- Establishing strategic leadership with DEI characteristics

- Evolution of emotional intelligence practices for leadership development

- Factors for institutionalizing DEI changes

- Development of a DEI performance management plan

Who can benefit from this book?

This book was created to provide an educational resource for multiple groups of people including:

- Senior, C-Suite, and human professionals who want to create a DEI Management plan that will enhance their opportunity to create a motivated and productive workforce

- Students studying business management or human management - This book will serve as a practical hands-on manual for learning about DEI initiatives and the importance of leaders' emotional intelligence mindset to create these opportunities for their workforce.

- DEI consultants or community leaders - This book will provide real-life applications on how to develop an effective DEI Plan for hiring, engagement, and leader development purposes.

- And the general public to become aware of the positive effects that DEI has in creating a more desirable product for their consumption.

This page is intentionally left blank

How to use this book?

- This book can be used as a desk guide and educational reference in understanding the effects that DEI plays in the development of organizational leaders, and employees, and the creation of standard operational procedures.

- This book provides a theoretical perspective of how when used correctly and strategically, DEI can enhance the connection and build synergy with the internal and external customers associated with the sustainability of the company.

- For business, community, and human resource professionals/leaders, this book will provide a blueprint of how to create a DEI plan and how to recognize a need for institutionalized change. In addition, this book will provide a bird's-eye view of the never-ending possibilities organizations can achieve with the insertion of DEI initiatives as a part of their core competencies or strategic plan.

- This book is an introduction to understanding that DEI is a proactive movement in the world of business that offers countless opportunities for organizations to be relevant in their industries, and be accountable to their prospective stakeholders.

This page is intentionally left blank

Chapter 1

Understanding Diversity, Equity, and Inclusion and Determining Why You Need Distributed Leadership

This chapter will clearly define the meaning of diversity, equity, and inclusion (DEI). DEI will be described as a mindset and proactive action that was initiated by organizational leaders to create a harmonious, equal, and equitable workplace environment where everyone could excel in their particular position. In addition, this chapter will examine the highly controversial perspective of DEI initiatives and the results of states in this country eliminating these efforts for equal opportunities.

Key learning objectives include the reader's understanding of the following:

- Definitions of the words diversity, equity, and inclusion

- Examining the historical implications of implementation of DEI initiatives into the workplace environment

- Understanding the social and political disagreements between state leaders and state lawmakers in agreeing to the basic principles of DEI programs

- Reexamining the consequences of eliminating DEI positions in organizations in the eradication of eliminating DEI being taught in higher education facilities

1.1 Defining What Diversity, Equity, and Inclusion Represents and the Significance of Introducing Distributed Leadership to Your Senior Leaders

Diversity, equity, and inclusion allow an organization to grow and attract multiverse talent. Diversity, equity, and inclusion are mindsets and leadership principles that enable a company to create a fair and equitable environment for all to grow and be productive in their positions. Organizational leaders' responsibilities are to foster and establish resources and a line of communication where everyone is heard and valued.

1.1.1 Diversity

Diversity speaks to identifying one's own bias and being able to manage one's own emotions to improve relationships with various groups and communities with the makeup of the organization's workforce. Organizational leaders must take into consideration demographic characteristics, cognitive differences, and cultural differences as elements of discussion when developing a welcoming work environment for all.

1. **Demographic characteristics** include race, ethnicity, gender, age, sexual orientation, disability status, socioeconomic status, nationality, religion, and language.

2. **Cognitive and experiential differences** include educational background, skills, knowledge, perspectives, and problem-solving approaches.

3. **Cultural and social differences** include values, beliefs, traditions, customs, and lifestyles.

Diversity allows employees to bring their unique personality and knowledge to the environment, which in turn makes them feel appreciated and respected. DEI is a mindset that has to be developed by both the employee and employer in order to create a welcoming environment. This welcoming environment will lead to a positive experience for the employee which will enhance a more productive and efficient outcome level. Organizational leaders, along with the human resource department, are responsible for incorporating DEI initiatives into the policies, processes, and daily work environment.

Diversity recognizes and values the unique contributions and perspectives that individuals from different backgrounds bring to a collective setting. Embracing diversity is not only about representation but also about creating environments where all individuals are respected, included, and empowered to participate fully and contribute their unique talents and insights. Diversity provides an organization the opportunity to use these cultural, social, and economic differences to develop a more comprehensive product or service that is going to be more representative and supported by external shareholders. Diversity allows an organization to tap into various areas of innovation and creativity by introducing new elements into its products or services.

1.1.2 Equity

According to Alfonseca (2023), "Equity focuses on fairness and justice, particularly referring to compensation and whether people are being paid or treated fairly". In other words, equity provides everyone inside an organization the same opportunity to be supported and to gain success in their respective positions. Equity is aimed at identifying the resources and information needed in order to maintain a level of equilibrium throughout the organization for all to be motivated and experience a sense of fulfillment in their designated role.

Equity allows an organization to achieve several important objectives such as:

1. **Enhancing talent perspectives and creating a potential talent pool:** Equity allows individuals with different educational backgrounds and work experiences to gain crucial learning opportunities and access to valuable resources throughout the organization. This initiative will allow the organization to foster current talent and create a pool of highly motivated and innovative talent.

2. **Development of workplace culture:** When employees are respected and supported by senior leadership, employees are more productive and engage in return-on-investment activities such as customer service and quality outcomes.

3. **Quality productivity and outcomes:** Human resource managers must work with senior leaders to create a

harmonious work environment where all employees can feel respected, and valued as shareholders in the organization. When employees feel empowered they will produce a higher level of quality organizational results and outcomes.

4. **Acquiring and keeping top talent:** Organizations have to advertise their vacancies in various avenues to attract a diversified hiring pool. Senior leaders must work with the human resource department to create equal opportunities for hiring and mentorship programs within the organization to establish equity and inclusion for all.

5. **Managing uncertainties and obstacles:** Creating DEI principles and policies within the organization can help eliminate potential lawsuits and reputational damage.

1.1.3 Inclusion

The final piece of DEI is inclusion. Inclusion is crafting a work environment in which each employee feels a sense of belonging and being an important part of generating a return on investment for their organization. Inclusion is inviting everyone to the strategic decision-making sessions and allowing each employee to provide personal insights on suggestions for improvements or relaying words of concern from various stakeholders involved in the day-to-day operations of the organization.

Inclusion is imperative for organizations to excel in their day-to-day operations for the following reasons:

1. **Diversity of a variety of viewpoints:** Organizations that incorporate inclusion bring innovative critical thinking

and increase decision-making opportunities into the environment. Ultimately, employees will be able to learn from their colleagues and develop a close-knit professional connection.

2. **A feeling of inclusion:** Inclusion allows everyone to be valued, heard, and respected. When this initiative is part of the work environment, senior leaders empower their employees to achieve greater job satisfaction and mastery.

3. **Fair access to opportunities:** Inclusive work environments allow everyone an equitable chance to achieve promotions, obtain training, and be accepted into the organization. Inclusion is a check and balance system to ensure everyone is adhering to the principles of equal opportunity access for all.

4. **Improved efficiency and output:** Organizations that develop inclusion practices will enable their employees to experience an increase in collaboration and productivity.

5. **Equitable treatment and justice:** Inclusion should emphasize the employee's right to fairness and equal opportunities inside the organization. Human resource managers must provide training for managers about the importance of promoting diversity and inclusion practices in their interactions with employees.

Overall, inclusion is important because it not only enriches organizational culture and performance but also reflects fundamental principles of fairness, respect, and equality. It creates environments where everyone has the opportunity to thrive and contribute their unique talents and perspectives.

1.1.4 Distributed leadership

For a company to be prosperous and victorious in today's competitive work environment, it must train its leaders to be transformational and visionary. A transformational leader is one who can build a transparent and honest professional relationship with their colleagues and the workforce. This initiative by the leader will convey a positive connotation of being able to obtain favorable outcome results. Leaders must understand how to use DEI initiatives to create evaluation practices into the organization's policies and procedures in learning how to support and provide crucial resources for increasing motivation and collaboration among employees.

In the 21st century, senior leaders need to establish DEI intelligence as part of an organizational statement that will set the tone about valuing diversity, equity, and inclusiveness for its employees to hear and feel. When organizations cultivate a positive work environment it values individual differences and creates a safe space where it can promote employer and employee relationships. All of this starts from the concept of "Distributed Leadership." Distributed leadership centers on accountability and developing collaborations with various entities inside the internal organization. This type of leadership is also known as shared leadership. Where trust and employee empowerment can be enhanced to allow everyone to contribute to achieving the organization's strategic goals.

Distributed leadership is a framework that was refined by scholar James Spillane (2005). As a leadership theory, distributed leadership reflects a growing recognition of the importance of collaboration, shared decision-making, and collective responsibility in contemporary organizations. Distributed leadership is a management theory that relies on teamwork and shared decision-making opportunities. This theory taps into the various talents of the team members' capability to come up with solutions to achieve goal-oriented success.

Distributed leadership is important in understanding DEI for several reasons:

1. **It promotes diverse perspectives:** By involving a broad range of individuals in leadership roles, distributed leadership ensures that diverse perspectives and experiences are represented in decision-making processes. This helps to prevent the marginalization of certain groups and ensures that the needs and interests of all stakeholders are considered.

2. **It strengthens collaboration and inclusivity:** Distributed leadership fosters a culture of collaboration, cooperation, and inclusivity, where everyone is encouraged to participate and contribute their unique skills and insights. This helps to create a sense of ownership and investment among team members, leading to greater engagement and commitment to DEI initiatives.

3. **It empowers grassroots initiatives**: Distributed leadership empowers individuals and teams at all levels of the organization to take ownership of DEI initiatives and drive change from the bottom up. This allows for more flexibility, adaptability, and responsiveness to the specific needs and challenges faced by different departments or groups within the organization.

4. **It builds capacity for change**: By distributing leadership responsibilities across the organization, DEI efforts can be more sustainable and scalable over time. Distributed leadership builds capacity for change by developing leadership skills and capabilities among a wider pool of individuals, ensuring that DEI becomes embedded into the organizational culture and practices.

Distributed leadership is important in understanding DEI because it promotes collaboration, inclusivity, and empowerment, which are essential principles for creating diverse, equitable, and inclusive organizations. By distributing leadership responsibilities, organizations can harness the collective talents and efforts of their entire workforce to drive meaningful change and advance DEI goals (Leithwood, Mascall, Strauss, 2009).

1.2 The Emergence of DEI Practices in Corporate Settings

DEI (Diversity, Equity, and Inclusion) practices in corporate settings are crucial for fostering a workplace culture that values and respects all employees regardless of their background, identity, or characteristics. The emergence of DEI practices first flourished as part of the Civil Rights Movement in the 1950s and 1960s. This movement brought societal and legal changes recognizing that systemic discrimination needed to be eradicated on the basis of race, color, religion, sex, and national origin.

By the early 1970s, affirmative action policies were introduced to address historical discrimination and promote equal opportunity in employment and education. These policies aimed to increase the representation and participation of underrepresented groups, including racial minorities, women, and individuals with disabilities, in workplaces and educational institutions. According to Ferguson (2014), "Affirmative action policies were established by Presidents John F. Kennedy and Lyndon B. Johnson to forbid discriminatory hiring practices in regard to race, religion, gender and country of origin". Affirmative actions were deemed necessary to hold leaders in organizations accountable for supplying equitable and fair opportunities internally. These opportunities included such activities as recruiting, in-house training programs, and equal pay necessities.

When the 1980s and 1990s arrived, organizations not only had to worry about competing domestically but for the first time we began to hear the word "globalization". Globalization was a crucial step organization leaders had to visualize in order to be relevant in their current industry. The increasing globalization of economies and the movement of people across borders have led to more diverse workforces in many countries. As organizations expanded their operations globally, they encountered diverse cultures, perspectives, and talent pools, prompting the need for more inclusive workplace practices. Globalization created a need for organizational leaders to have a greater understanding of cultural differences and nuances in communication, behavior, and business practices.

As the country entered the 21st century, consumers fought for social and cultural movements. Inclusion and representation of all groups in society, especially in the workplace spurred organizations to rethink their policies and hiring practices. Ultimately prompting leaders to create a culture where all could belong and be given an opportunity to succeed. DEI initiatives became a pertinent action that organizational leaders had to begin to prioritize in leading a diverse workforce for increased profit and innovation capabilities.

Due to demographic shifts of minority groups, especially the Latino population, and the intergenerational changes in the workforce, organizational leaders had to adjust their group-think way of thinking and expand into attracting and retaining talent from various ethnic backgrounds to remain competitive in this rapidly changing global marketplace. Finally, DEI practices in corporate settings have emerged as a response to societal pressures, economic struggles, and progressing attitudes toward diversity, equity, and inclusion.

1.3 Exploring the Evolution of DEI Adoption Among Employers

The early DEI adoption is broken up into 4 stages: early stage, mid-stage, current stage, and future stage. These stages are important in putting historical content into place as they correlate to the mindsets of social and organizational perspectives on DEI initiatives. During the early stage which is described as the awareness and recognition stage, affirmative action and other crucial employment legislation was enacted by Congress to bring discrimination and racism to the forefront of workplace laws and practices. In the mid-stage, which is the legal mandates stage, diversity training programs were initiated in corporate America to address equal employment initiatives The current stage, which is the third stage, addressed organizational accountability in providing leadership development, hiring, and recruitment initiatives to attract diverse talent to organizations. For the first time, metrics and transparency were required to measure the effectiveness of these in-house diversity initiatives. Finally, the final stage is named as the future stage. During this stage employers realize by having a diverse workforce they could have a competitive advantage by offering a diverse portfolio which will lead to attracting various marginalized groups to their organization as customers. Given below is the synopsis of the main ideas of all four stages.

1. **Awareness and recognition (early stage)**:

   - In the early stages, employers began to recognize the importance of diversity in the workforce.

   - There was a growing awareness of the benefits of diversity for innovation, creativity, and market competitiveness.

   - Employers started to acknowledge the moral and business imperative of promoting diversity and inclusion.

2. **Compliance and legal mandates (mid stage)**:

   - As awareness grew, legal frameworks and regulations were established to address discrimination and promote diversity in the workplace.

   - Employers implemented diversity initiatives in response to legal requirements and regulatory mandates.

   - Diversity training programs and affirmative action policies became common strategies to ensure compliance with equal employment opportunity laws.

3. **Integration and strategic alignment (current stage):**

- In recent years, employers have shifted towards integrating DEI initiatives into their strategic business objectives.

- DEI is seen as a core component of organizational culture and values, rather than just a compliance issue.

- Employers are adopting holistic approaches to DEI that encompass recruitment, retention, leadership development, and organizational practices.

- There is a growing emphasis on metrics, accountability, and transparency in measuring the effectiveness of DEI efforts.

4. **Innovation and best practices (future stage):**

- The future evolution of DEI adoptions among employers is likely to involve a focus on innovation and best practices.

- Employers will continue to explore new approaches and strategies to enhance diversity, equity, and inclusion in the workplace.

- Collaboration and knowledge-sharing among organizations will drive the development of industry-wide standards and benchmarks for DEI excellence.

- DEI will be integrated into broader sustainability and corporate social responsibility initiatives, reflecting a holistic approach to organizational success.

DEI initiatives initially began as a way to recognize disparities in hiring practices and pay inequity discrepancies. A compatible way to address inequalities in the work and school environment. Now it has evolved into a mindset that organizations leaders have to possess to create a synergy to boost their bottom line. Through leadership DEI commitments, employees can improve their full potential which will motivate them to increase their productivity rate.

DEI cannot be seen as an action to call out dominance and privilege but as a process to design a work environment where it is a safe place to share knowledge and feedback from the various stakeholders to format a win-win collaboration for the success of the day-to-day operations of the organization. So therefore, the evolution of DEI adoptions among employers reflects a progression from basic awareness and compliance to strategic integration and innovation, with a growing emphasis on organizational values, culture, and business impact.

To conclude, due to the evolution of DEI adoption, many employers have started incorporating unconscious bias training and organizing cultural competency workshops. Companies have begun refining their DEI policies to ensure equal opportunities in recruitment, retention, and promotion, as well as creating safe spaces for marginalized groups. They are developing measurable metrics that monitor hiring and retention statistics, and promotion numbers. All of these steps hold leaders accountable for their progression in achieving the organizations' DEI goals set forth. Finally, a competitive sustainable organization understands that DEI work is ongoing and requires continuous improvement, by regularly reviewing and updating its strategies to address evolving challenges and opportunities internally and externally.

1.4 Examining the Social and Political Controversies Surrounding DEI as Leaders and Lawmakers Clash

During the height of the COVID-19 health pandemic, due to the social and racial unrest in the United States, organizations began to reevaluate their policies for improving the representation of under-marginalized groups in their workforce. Taylor and Mark (2024) of the "Washington Post" believe that many conservative organizations looked at DEI programs or initiatives as discriminatory principles created to give non-caucasian groups advantages. These executives fail to realize that DEI fosters a welcoming environment where everyone from all socio/economic, and racial statuses has an opportunity to be respected and express their ideas and perspectives freely.

Stemming from the Supreme Court's decision, controversies begin to commence around the use of quotas and DEI initiatives. Political lawmakers became convinced that DEI initiatives and quotas led to window dressing for hiring opportunities and resulted in qualified applicants who were not minorities becoming overlooked in this process. Meanwhile, proponents assert that DEI Initiatives are crucial for promoting significant transformation inside these brick-and-mortar institutions.

DEI initiatives frequently encompass advocating for inclusive language and confronting offensive or discriminatory speech. Nonetheless, discussions surrounding political correctness and freedom of speech rights can generate tensions, as some contend that DEI efforts constrain freedom of expression or hinder open dialogue. Businesses that publicly advocate for DEI causes or participate in activism could encounter criticism from customers, staff, or political figures. Detractors allege that corporations practice "social justice branding" to prioritize symbolic gestures over substantive progress, whereas proponents contend that companies bear a responsibility to leverage their impact for societal benefits. Social justice branding led to criticism of diversity training, where many state legislators voiced displeasure with these training initiatives. Critics affirmed that such programs were ineffective and nurtured a victim mentality or incited resentment among employees, whereas proponents greatly believe that these training programs enhanced an organization's ability to foster cultural competency and alleviate discrimination.

The purpose of the DEI movement was to shed light on the inequalities in the workplace for women and minorities. This movement started back in the mid-1960s as a call for social justice. During this time laws were introduced into society such as equal employment and affirmative action laws. These laws initiated the concept of workplace diversity training.

The DEI movement moved from focusing on racial discriminatory practices to targeting a wider spectrum of diversity initiatives. For the first time, the DEI movement identified groups of individuals based on ethnicity, religion, and sexual orientation communities. This created a shift of thought from confrontational to transformational thinking. Ultimately, it is important to define the roles of leaders in organizations to understand the crucial role they play in creating policies to enhance business and organizational effectiveness.

In the 1980s and 1990s, the DEI movement witnessed the emergence of diversity professionals inside the organizations. This action alone created a monumental visual for organizational leaders to explore diversity as a key driver for success instead of looking at diversity as a moral dilemma. As we moved into the 21st century, the DEI movement began to integrate social media into taking action and recognizing the social and political connections to DEI.

1.5 Impact of Removing DEI Initiatives from Workplaces and Higher Education

The impact of eliminating DEI initiatives in our society could hinder the progression of creating a similar playing field for men versus women, black versus white, and other minorities. Potential elimination of DEI initiatives from higher universities could result in losses of student support services. For example, students with disabilities might not be able to access accommodations deemed necessary to support their learning opportunities in higher education. In addition, eliminating DEI initiatives in higher education will create a difficult task for higher education administrators to recruit and retain talented minority faculty. Finally, minorities who only can gain access to higher education through sporting scholarships could lose this incredible opportunity to obtain education to eliminate generational poverty within their families and communities.

Elimination of DEI efforts inside higher educational institutions will enable students with disabilities and first-time generational students to be blocked from receiving student support services that impact them in being successful in and out of the classroom. These support services include tutoring and academic assistance, internship, and work-study opportunities for preparation for life after college. Grantors who firmly believe in DEI initiatives might stop partnering up with these higher education institutions which will hinder various internal progress, such as recruiting qualified minority faculty and students. Eradication of DEI focus on campuses across the country will have a more difficult time in continuing to work on sustainable solutions for student safety. This alone will lead to an unhealthy campus environment where everyone's voice and presence are not valued or respected.

As far as the workplace goes, the elimination of DEI perspectives will result in lower creativity, lower employee engagement, lower profitability, and a groupthink mentality. Ultimately this will have a heavy effect on a company trying to turn a positive ROI (Return on Investments) for the organization. Inclusive work environments allow employees to create a better comprehensive product for the customer. This can only occur when diverse teams are created internally to be a part of the solution and creation process. Organizations that work with the HR department and senior leaders to create an inclusive internal environment are more likely to enhance a stronger connection with their employees. Connectivity is an important element of creating a bond between employer and employee, which in business terms stops employees from leaving organizations at a higher pace. As shown in Figure 1.1, the Pew Research Center conducted a survey in February 2023, that asked random workers if they believe implementation of DEI initiatives is important in workplace environments. 56% of workers surveyed thought this was a great component to insert.

Figure 1.1 **Pew Research Center DEI survey results (February 2023)**

A majority of workers say focusing on DEI at work is a good thing

% of employed adults saying that in general, focusing on increasing diversity, equity and inclusion at work is mainly ...

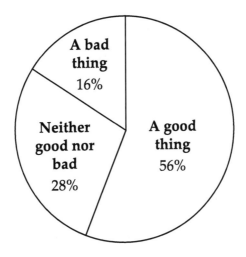

Note: Based on workers who are not self-employed and work at a company or organization with 10 or more people. Share of respondents who didn't offer an answer (<0.5%) not shown.

Source: Survey of U.S. workers conducted Feb. 6-12, 2023, "Diversity, Equity, and Inclusion in the Workplace", Pew Research Center, https://www.pewresearch.org

Finally, it is important to understand that DEI initiatives play a crucial role in supporting the success of underrepresented students in higher education. By providing resources, support networks, and opportunities for academic and professional development, these initiatives help mitigate the barriers and challenges that underrepresented students may face. Removing DEI initiatives can worsen existing disparities in retention, graduation rates, and post-graduation outcomes. Without the support and resources provided by DEI initiatives, underrepresented students may struggle to navigate the academic environment, access essential support services, and develop the skills and networks needed for success. As a result, it's essential for higher education institutions to recognize the importance of DEI initiatives and to continue investing in them to ensure that all students have equal opportunities to thrive and succeed.

As far as eliminating DEI initiatives in the workplace is concerned, it can have negative implications. Organizations that disregard DEI efforts can create an unfair workplace environment where employees do not value or feel a sense of appreciation. This will lead to unproductive outcomes and a lower degree of job gratification. Furthermore, companies that do not embrace diversity will not benefit from a larger talent pool to attract top candidates.

Chapter 2

Diversity, Equity, and Inclusion in Employment Opportunities

Diversity is the ability of an organization to create best practices that allow for setting realistic goals and the understanding of acceptance of someone's physical and mental capabilities or differences. When organizations include DEI policies as part of their day-to-day protocols, it ensures everyone feels safe to express their identity without fear of discrimination or harassment.

When equity and inclusion are present in the workplace it provides a positive mindset and change to the company. Equal opportunities in the workplace can only occur when workers feel supported and respected by their peers and employers. Support in the sense of allowing the employees to voice their ideas and opinions regardless of position held inside the organization. Integration becomes a key terminology in promoting equity and diversity in the workplace.

In Chapter 2, we will be looking at various ways in which organizational leaders can promote DEI in the workplace by creating policies that are committed to diversity, equity, and inclusion. We will also take a look at ways to educate leaders on how to foster inclusive communications with their employees to ensure everyone is valued and respected throughout the organization. Finally, to understand the composition of their workforce and the needs of the different groups identified inside the organization.

Key learning objectives include the reader's understanding of the following:

- Incorporating diversity and inclusion into the workplace structure

- Acknowledging and valuing diversity, equity, and inclusion attributes among individuals, teams, and organizational personnel

- Understanding the competitive advantage provided by diversity, equity, and inclusion initiatives within organizational structures

- Learning how senior leaders execute strategies within the organizational framework to promote diversity, equity, and inclusion

- Creating the role of a DEI officer tasked with formulating corporate policies

Figure 2.1 displays the definitions of what diversity, equity and inclusion can bring into the workplace environment. DEI initiatives create a win-win situation from both the employer's and employee's perspective. By creating an inclusive DEI workplace environment, organizational leaders help increase employee engagement and retention. When this state of euphoria is present in the workplace, employees can produce more efficient and reliable results. These results are based on the development of transparency and trust established in the communication between employer and employee.

Figure 2.1	Definition of diversity, equity, and inclusion

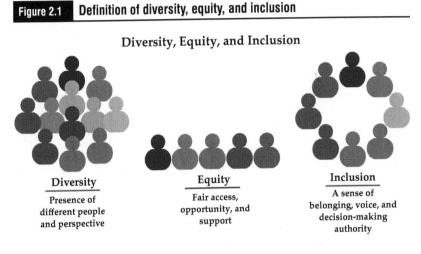

Diversity, Equity, and Inclusion

Diversity	Equity	Inclusion
Presence of different people and perspective	Fair access, opportunity, and support	A sense of belonging, voice, and decision-making authority

Source: Adapted from Open Oregon Educational Resources, https://openoregon. pressbooks.pub

2.1 Extent of Incorporating Diversity and Inclusion into the Workplace Structure

In the 21st-century workplace environment, organizational leaders have to focus on diversity and inclusion as an initiative to employ a more diversified staff to assist them in providing an effective product that reflects the society in which they serve. This means that organizations have to adopt DEI (diversity, equity, and inclusion)strategies that allow employees to stay connected and productive in their positions.

Many organizations are clearly stumped about how to measure the effects DEI initiatives can bring to the organization's workforce environment. In order to obtain a better insight into this, the following components will be examined:

1. Organizational culture

2. Metrics

3. D&I policies and best practices

4. Leadership dedication and responsibility

5. Analysis and assessment

6. External stakeholder involvement

These six fundamental principles of incorporating diversity and inclusion in the workplace will serve as a framework for human resource managers to use in changing the condition of the current workplace structure as we see it now.

2.1.1 Organizational culture

Figure 2.2   **Edgar Schein's organizational model**

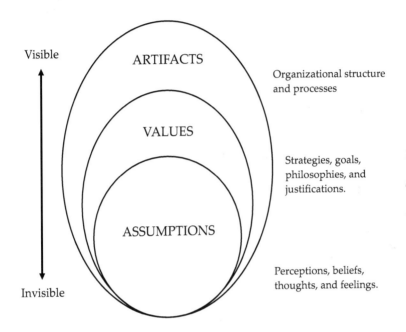

Figure 2.2 displays Edgar Schein's (1995) organizational model. Schein terms organizational culture as the artifacts of the organization, that is, the beliefs and values the organization treasures. Based on Edgar Schien's "organizational culture" model there are three levels: artifacts, espoused values, and underlying assumptions. Artifacts are derived from the visible signs that employees observe on a daily basis as being a part of the organizational workforce. These visible signs provide employees with the expectations that the organization expects their employees to be able to act in the organization, such as dress codes and the design of the interior layout of the employees' workplace. According to Schein, these do nothing to make an impact on organizational culture. The second phase of Schein's

organizational culture model is named espoused values. During this phase, employees examine how employees react to the organizational culture. In other words, how does the organization influence the culture of the organization? This is the phase where employees begin to describe how the organization treats them; such as how the employees value the mission, vision, and goals developed by the organization. The final stage of the model is described as the underlying assumptions level. At the underlying assumptions level is where employees perceive and interact with the culture This level influences how employees approach their daily jobs and how they value their job performance. Underlying assumptions can be described by employees' unconscious perceptions feelings and values they hold about the company. Finally, underlying assumptions are the key element in the model with respect to being able to observe how employees learn and share knowledge with others in the organization to foster a positive organizational culture.

Schein believes that an employee has to fully support and value their employer in order to be satisfied with their work and produce at a valiant outcome level. When employees are unable to adjust to their work environment and garner a negative mindset to the organizational structure, their work productivity level falters.

The famous quote "culture eats strategy for breakfast" indicates that organizations must create a culture that is engaging and empowering. Create a culture that is flexible and innovative where employees can be responsible for outcome results.

2.1.2 Metrics

D& I metrics are correlated to the efforts your organization has placed to measure accountability and how successful or not they have been in coordinating fairness and employee satisfaction. Hewlin (2019) described several ways that organizations can use DEI metrics to measure their progression:

1. **Demographics** - Demographics are important to measure the diversification level of employees at various levels across the organization. To do this you would divide the number of people in a particular demographic group by the total population.

2. **Retention rate** - This data will assist leaders in understanding retention issues with various groups of employees inside the organization. This specific metric can be calculated as follows:

   Total number of employees in the organization – Total number of employees in the specific group you are measuring/ Total number of employees x 100.

3. **Employee advancement or promotion rate** - To calculate this you would use:

   The number of employees promoted in a specific group / Total headcount.

4. **Equal pay and pay equity** - This metric will assist with uncovering potential issues with pay practices inside the organization. For example; to calculate to see if there is a gender gap, you will need to calculate the average hourly pay of male employees and female employees, and divide it by the number of male employees. This process would be duplicated with the female employees. Then you would

subtract the average female hourly rate versus the average male hourly pay rate, divided by the average hourly pay rate for males multiplied by 100.

DEI metrics allow senior leaders an opportunity to continuously measure how effectively identify biases and gain an understanding of how fairness and equitable components are being introduced into the work environment.

Overall, Hewlin's work underscores the importance of robust measurement systems and data-driven approaches in advancing diversity and inclusion efforts within organizations.

2.1.3 Inclusive policies and practices

Jennifer Brown, who is the author of two books "Inclusion: Diversity, The New Workplace & The Will to Change" (2016) and "How to Be an Inclusive Leader: Your Role in Creating Cultures of Belonging Where Everyone Can Thrive," (2019) examines the critical ways that organizational leaders can encompass DEI initiatives inside their workplace.

The ways you can incorporate inclusive policies and best practices inside the workplace is by implementing the following components:

1. **Practicing promoting inclusive environments:** This involves recognizing and challenging one's biases, and learning how to receive critical feedback from others. In addition, leaders need to communicate clearly and respectfully through appropriate dialogue. Finally, coming up with social events to celebrate differences as a way to bring acceptance and empowerment into the organization's culture is also involved.

2. **Fostering diversity:** Organizational leaders need to invest in mentorship programs that will allow women and minorities an opportunity to grow into senior leadership positions. Another way to foster diversity is to create a DEI hiring committee. The hiring committee will interview potential candidates of various sexual orientations, social and educational experiences, and ethnic compositions for filling vacancies in the organizations.

3. **Ensuring leadership precision:** This is the ability to influence others' behaviors to accept inclusive policies and practices when it comes to respecting and valuing others around them. It is important to be transparent in building a rapport with the employees to increase employee engagement and success in achieving designated strategic goals for the organization.

4. **Elimination of biases:** Employees and employers must be self-cognizant of their implicit biases and reflect on their own personal interactions with others in the workplace. Admit mistakes and be open to honest feedback from colleagues who have witnessed your unconscious bias being displayed at work.

5. **Promoting employee resource groups (ERGs):** These groups can offer professional development, and cultural awareness to their members through creating a sense of community and access to decision-makers in the organization. They allow employees to engage in conversations with others who are experiencing similar conflicts and develop friendships with others in the same ethnic groups.

2.1.4 Leadership dedication and responsibilities

Simon Sinek (2014) who is an inspirational speaker on business leadership believes that leaders have to listen to their employees' viewpoints to obtain a different perspective of the temperature inside the work environment. In other words, leaders must trust their employees' ability to be committed to fulfilling the mission and vision of the organization. Leaders must build a relationship with their employees to develop loyalty, trust, and collaboration.

2.1.5 Analysis and assessment

Organizations that are truly concerned with assessing diversity and inclusion inside their organization will make sure to establish their DEI goals with the organization's mission and vision statement. Conduct employee surveys to obtain critical feedback on what is working and what needs improvement inside the organization. Finally, compare and contrast their organization's DEI goals against their industry DEI benchmark requirements.

2.1.6 External stakeholder involvement

Organizational leaders need to make sure that they set goals and establish a certain awareness of inclusion from all stakeholder groups. Include underrepresented groups as part of your stakeholders to obtain a different viewpoint for outcome results. Identify who are the groups that will be impacted or can have a positive impact on your organization's bottom line. Finally, analyze your stakeholders to have a clearer understanding of their specific needs to be met by the organization.

2.2 Recognizing Diversity, Equity, and Inclusion Traits Across Individuals Teams, and Organizational Staff

For organizations to recognize diversity, equity, and inclusion traits across individual teams and organizational staff, it must start with a top-down, bottom-up strategy. Top-down, bottom-up strategy is when organizational decisions are made only by senior executives at the hierarchy level. While bottom-up strategy occurs where all managers from all different levels of the organization can be involved in the decision-making process. This type of strategy is how communications are distributed inside the organization where activities are discussed surrounding the implementation.

Leaders must be fully committed to implementing DEI initiatives throughout the organization, starting with actively engaging the senior leaders and enhancing employee involvement in communicating about diversity and inclusion inside the work environment and what it should feel and look like. Both the employer and employee should take the time to understand the goals and vision of the organization and how it can correlate to the overall business objectives. Each person has to fully realize how DEI impacts their position within the organization.

As employees, they can initiate Employee Resource Groups or become actively involved in serving on crucial internal committees. Everyone inside the organization needs to become more culturally competent. The HR manager needs to push for socially conscious activities to occur inside the organization where employees can learn and appreciate their colleagues of various backgrounds, and cultures. In addition, the HR manager needs to incorporate various training to assist in developing cultural sensitivity and diversity awareness inside the work environment. Furthermore, create diversity policies and principles that can drive a positive change in mindset within the organization. Finally, HR along with the senior leaders of organizations have to be proactive in incorporating fair promotion practices to increase the visibility of women and other marginalized individuals with the opportunity to move up the corporate ladder through mentorship programs.

As an HR consultant, for years I have known the positive impact that diversity and inclusion have in the transformation of the organization's policies and practices. In other words, DEI initiatives help an organization tailor its organizational strategy, values, and culture to the needs of its stakeholders. By looking at talent identification, leadership development, employee engagement, and training and development, organizations can use data analytics to assist them in advancing DEI initiatives properly within the internal environment of their organizations.

In 2013, Dr. Bernardo Ferdman co-authored a book entitled, "Diversity at Work: The Practice of Inclusion". The book focused on why diversity and inclusion should matter for organizations and how to foster diversity and inclusion.

Ferdman created a strategic model for inclusion called, "Multilevel Analytic Framework." This framework is a step-by-step guide on how to introduce inclusion into the organization as part of their strategies, policies, procedures, and mindset on their day-to-day operational activities. Ferdman (2023) believed that the main duty of the organization leaders was to create ways to ensure that employees feel accepted and connected to the mission and vision of the organization. It's up to the leaders to support and assist their employees in maintaining their unique identities and culture while operating within the context of their positions within the organization. To support this logical thought process, inclusion surveys need to be given to employees to measure the progression of DEI initiatives that must be implemented inside the organization. Finally, for D&I to be relevant inside the organization the talent management process must be correlated to building a strong relationship between job opportunities for movement up the corporate ladder and creating a linear line on having a profitable business result.

Embracing diversity, equity, and inclusion across individuals, teams, and organizational staff demands a comprehensive strategy that includes fostering awareness, appreciating diverse perspectives, promoting inclusive leadership, implementing fair practices, nurturing collaborative teamwork, and cultivating a supportive organizational climate. By prioritizing these elements, organizations can establish environments where every individual feels esteemed, appreciated, and empowered to excel.

2.3 Gaining Insight Into the Competitive Edge Offered by Diversity, Equity, and Inclusion Initiatives in Organizational Frameworks

In today's fast-paced and competitive domestic and global market, companies must continue to push the envelope in creating more innovative products and executing superb customer services. Diversity and Inclusion initiatives can assist an organization in improving brand loyalty, and employee satisfaction, and increase innovative stimulation. DEI allows organizations to reexamine their companies' culture, and hiring practices and check the mindset of their employees' well-being. Companies that embrace DEI instead of avoiding it can gain a competitive advantage by fostering a more inclusive and supported working and learning environment.

In this section of the chapter, I will delve into the multiple perspectives of how DEI can create a positive impact on increasing the bottom line numbers of an organization. Let's look at the perspective of innovation. Innovation through creating diverse teams allows a company to offer a more comprehensive product that entails ideas of various individuals with different education, life, and work experiences, ultimately leading to a more creative and efficient product. Another way to gain a competitive edge with DEI is through increasing employee engagement and job satisfaction. The HR department must create a work environment where employees can share their ideas and express their opinions without any negative recourse. In addition, employees must be able to gain access to valuable organizational resources such as training, and mentorship programs for personal growth development. These types of programs will lead to employee engagement and increase job satisfaction, which will equally increase productivity outcomes. Finally, implementing DEI initiatives will lead to increased revenue growth, increased competitiveness within the industry, and more smart brand appeal. Remember, society is more likely to support a company that is committed to diversity and inclusion: which can be linked to the values of the people the organization serves.

2.4 Implementing Organizational Strategies to Foster Diversity, Equity, and Inclusion in the Organizational Framework

Implementing DEI strategies into companies' core competencies and organizational framework can create a work environment that incorporates differences in values and beliefs and reflects the unique demographic and socio-economic characteristics of their workforce. As indicated throughout this chapter when a company invests in its employee's well-being and professional growth the organization's ROI (Return on Investments) can skyrocket. In order for companies to take advantage of DEI initiatives they must incorporate strategies internally. According to Bhasin (2017), leaders must be able to become champions and be proactive in enhancing D&I efforts inside the organization. This effort can be initiated by including diversity and inclusion in all business activities. Activities such as developing relationships with minority suppliers and distributors will portray a more authentic public image of the company being active in promoting inclusion. Furthermore, creating diverse teams inside the organization will create products and services that attract a diverse clientele. Developing training will address unconscious biases and how we recognize them. Stakeholders must hold senior leaders in organizations in implementing D&I initiatives as part of their core business strategies.

In 2016, Bourke wrote a book entitled, "Why Diversity and Inclusion Matter: Financial Performance", indicating that lack of diversity, equity, and inclusion is expensive for organizations. No matter what metric analysis you use, a lack of diversity, equity, and inclusion limits national economies and reduces the Gross Domestic Product of the country. This indicates that companies suffer a lack of innovation and creativity, weaker revenues, cash flow opportunities, and lower employee retention rates. As a society, the lack of DEI initiatives impacts educational outcomes, physical and mental health, lifetime achievement earnings, and generosity of wealth. DEI is congruent with innovation and growth. Creating a DEI workplace culture facilitates employee's willingness to learn and develop innovative capabilities. In addition, innovation translates to economic stability and competitive sustainability where employees learn how to make better decisions which leads to increased revenue and productivity outcomes. To summarize, senior leaders need to be held accountable for the implementation of DEI initiatives throughout all levels of the company to have a significant impact on the financial stability of the company's survival rate in the industry or with the support of its customer base.

2.5 Establishing the Position of a DEI Officer to Craft Corporate Policies

In order for organizations to maintain consistency in dedicating their mission and vision to DEI initiatives they have to create vital positions such as Chief Diversity Officer (CDO), Chief Culture Officer (CCO), or Chief DEI Officer (CDEIO). These positions are relevant in assisting organizational leaders in enforcing pay equality, and promotional opportunities to women and minorities. In addition, individuals who occupy these critical roles in the organization are responsible for developing company policies and practices that ensure everyone is valued and respected within the workplace.

Many DEI employees facilitate reviewing existing data on how the company is meeting its DEI benchmarks as well as redeveloping the appropriate inclusive language that should be included in job descriptions. Furthermore, Chief DEI Officers are held accountable by their stakeholders to conduct various DEI training for the senior leaders and employees of the organization. The main purpose of establishing the positions of DEI officers is to make sure companies are addressing any structural inequalities in the organization and to create a "belonging" work environment where employees can be themselves without fear of being punished or shunned by their colleagues.

It is important to acknowledge that the publicity of racially motivated crimes occurring outside organizations has created a mindset shift from a society where leaders should play an active role in addressing discrimination and inequities. With this in mind, D&I initiatives have been increasing rapidly within organizations leadership scope. DEI has gone from being a legal requirement to a critical business driver that influences financial and talent outcomes. Senior leaders now understand that diversity and inclusion is a huge competitive advantage factor in profitability. D&I roles in organizations are critical in eliminating hierarchies within the internal structures and setting clear goals and vision from a strategic viewpoint.

This page is intentionally left blank

Chapter 3

Fostering Organizational Culture and Enacting Strategic Leadership Initiatives

Organizational leaders in today's fast-paced work environment have to be transformational and situational leaders. These leaders have to be visionary and proactive in shaping corporate values and laying the principles of business strategies. To foster organizational culture, senior leaders have to clearly communicate the core values and goals and define expectations they have from every stakeholder that is associated with the sustainability of the organization. In a strategic sense, the organization must hire individuals who are not only qualified but also fit the company's culture. Furthermore, senior leaders must lead by example in setting the appropriate behavior and work ethic that is required by employees to be deemed successful in their positions. Senior leaders should encourage diverse teams' collaboration in solving problems or creating a new product. Lastly, for an organization to foster culture, it must empower its employees through designated training and employee recognition ceremonies.

When you foster organizational culture, you establish strategic initiatives that are set to achieve specific goals or to measure the overall effectiveness of your organization's ability to meet the needs of its customers and the industry market and be competitive with its competitors. This means being proactive in engaging with employees at all levels of the organization and monitoring the internal and external environment for emerging trends. Lastly, it also involves enhancing opportunities and being able to respond rapidly to challenges the organization is currently facing or will face in the future.

Key learning objectives include the reader's understanding of the following:

- Clarifying the resilience and diversity of organizational culture

- The five methods leaders can use to shape and cultivate organizational culture

- Recognizing different strategic leadership approaches to drive DEI structural transformations

- Implementing emotional intelligence strategies to embed DEI policies and processes across internal and external environments

- Acknowledging the requirement to institutionalize DEI transformations

3.1 Resilience and Diversity of Organizational Culture

Figure 3.1   **Resilience and diversity framework**

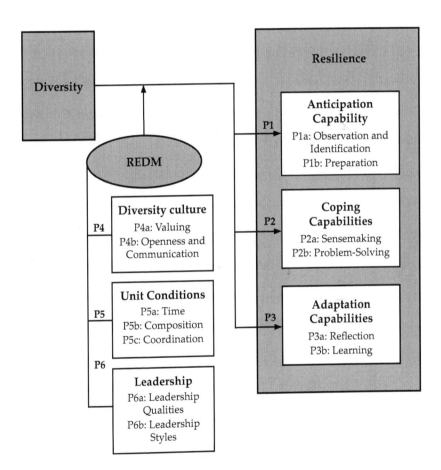

Source: Duchek, S., Raetze, S., & Scheuch, I. (2020). The role of diversity in organizational resilience: A theoretical framework. *Business Research, 13*(2), 387–423. https://doi.org/10.1007/s40685-019-0084-8

Figure 3.1 describes the resilience and diversity framework. This framework describes resilience as the capability to deal with any adverse events that occur outside that have a major impact on the internal work environment. The second part of the framework under "diversity culture" lists the two most crucial elements a company must recognize as part of the diverse work units inside the organizational culture: openness and communication and the conceptual value senior executives place on diversity inside the organization. Based on this concept, if employees feel valued and supported in their view of diversity initiatives being implemented inside the organization, then they are more likely to produce a higher productivity rate which will assist the organization to have a competitive advantage over their competitors. Openness and communication in the context of Figure 3.1 shown above indicate that these two attributes play a huge part in the unit conditions. If unit conditions are done correctly, knowledge sharing occurs which creates a positive outcome for the members in that unit.

As we dissect the various components of the resilience and diversity framework let's look at the REDM (resilience, equity, diversity, and management) elements: P4: "Diversity", P5: "Unit conditions", and P6: "Leadership". P here stands for "propositions" REDM helps organizations adapt to challenges that occur internally and externally in the workplace environment. Senior executives include DEI initiatives to make equitable and fair decisions that lead to a more sustainable execution of day-to-day operational activities that reflect all stakeholders' perspectives which helps build resilience. In the resilience and diversity management (REDM) framework, the first section, P4: "Diversity culture," emphasizes the importance of participation as a key element of organizational resilience and employee engagement. Diversity culture is congruent to participation. In order to build resilience and employee engagement. Organizations must incorporate people from all walks of life to share their perspectives on problem-solving capabilities and innovation opportunities. The second section is P5: "Unit conditions." Unit conditions focus on protection. HR managers along with senior executives must incorporate policies, and procedures that allow for all groups and individuals present in the workforce to have the opportunity, resources, and support to be successful inside the organizational structure. The final section of the resilience and diversity management framework is P6: "Leadership." This final section is geared toward collecting data and being transparent in terms of promotion. Promotions can be identified and reported on the annual DEI reports where all stakeholders involved with the successful operations of the organization can see the organization's efforts in meeting these particular goals and objectives as part of the strategic plan.

Leadership styles and quality play a definite role in developing a cohesive and inclusive organizational culture. Democratic leadership where empowerment and teamwork foster a culture that will continue to improve and possess the ability to be creative.

The final stage or section of the resilience and diversity framework discusses the following components: anticipation capabilities, coping capabilities, and adaptation capabilities. Anticipation capabilities is the initial stage in describing organizational resilience. This stage determines how organizations react or forecast an unexpected event. Organizations that can easily adapt to these unforeseen events are able to minimize potential losses. Coping capabilities refer to senior executives' ability to provide emotional support and establish resources in order for them to deal with this unforeseen event affecting the workplace environment. Finally, adaptation capabilities involve how well the organizational structure will be able to cope with this unforeseen event and be able to see an opportunity in this situation.

Organizations have to continuously mitigate the risk to their workforce and the condition of their internal system's ability to be effective in a crisis. In order to strengthen organizational resilience, leaders must have a comprehensive outlook on how policies and processes such as technology and communications, and all internal departments can become more transparent. Technology and communications are important in an organizational culture because they allow the dissemination of information for employees to be able to make real-time decisions which can give the organization a competitive advantage in responding to the needs of their internal and external shareholders as the event unfolds.

Senior leaders must work with the various stakeholders in identifying internal and external improvements, where everyone is held accountable for understanding how to support the execution of achieving success in meeting the corporate objectives and goals. SWOT analysis should be done annually to determine where the organization is currently situated in understanding its workforce, processes, and technology ability to execute strategies in a timely manner.

Resilience is the ability of a company to create a systematic mindset where flexibility, agility, and the mental and physical well-being of the employee are taken into consideration. Senior leaders have to possess a selfless mentality to assist in developing a cohesive internal work environment. Organizations that understand their functionality to society have been able to capture internal growth and development since the COVID-19 health pandemic. These organizations have come out of the pandemic being able to quickly assess the needs of their customers and emerge as industry leaders. When organizations have resilience built into their framework, they can gain a competitive advantage by initiating knowledge-sharing technology and relevant performance reviews and creating an innovative work environment which leads to faster and more informed decision-making opportunities. Ultimately this leads to employees being able to adjust and learn quicker in a business challenge situation.

Figure 3.2 | **John Kotter's eight-step change model**

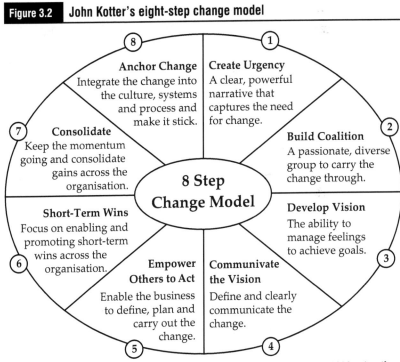

Source: *Kotter's 8-step change model—Easy walkthrough—Mutomorro*. (2023c, April 26). https://mutomorro.com/kotters-8-step-change-model/

In 1996, John Kotter developed his 8-step change model that focuses on organizational change. This model focuses on the following components: creating a sense of urgency, building a guiding coalition, forming a strategic vision, enlisting volunteers, enabling action by removing barriers, generating short-term wins, sustaining acceleration, and instituting change. Figure 3.2 lists John Kotter's 8-Step Change Model, which provides detailed steps that senior executives can implement to learn how to deal with obstacles inside their organizations. Ultimately, these steps provide a roadmap for allowing the organization to have sustainable growth.

Let's examine these components of Kotter's change model.

1. **Creating a sense of urgency:** Leaders must clearly communicate and provide a reason for the change. During this stage, employees have to be engaged in understanding the sense of urgency occurring within the organization.

2. **Building a guiding coalition:** The organization has to develop a coalition of senior leaders who their employees trust to follow during this time of chaos.

3. **Forming a strategic vision:** Senior leaders during this stage have to create a motivating and vibrant work environment where employees want to be. Specifically during the time of crisis, organizational leaders have to ensure their employees that this change will lead to a more profitable and sustainable future.

4. **Enlisting volunteers:** During this stage, senior leaders must identify employees who believe in this new change to support them in assisting their colleagues through this new organizational transition. These employees will be known as "change agents".

5. **Enabling action by removing barriers:** Senior leaders must identify internal factors that will reduce their opportunity

to not be successful. Once these obstacles are identified then senior leaders must provide adequate resources such as immediate training to deal with these newfound changes. In addition, constant communication must be prevalent to clarify why change is occurring inside the organization.

6. **Generating short-term wins:** Senior leaders should celebrate small victories with their employees. Remember, employees are more likely to be driven and cooperative in this transitional period when they are recognized and appreciated for their efforts.

7. **Sustaining acceleration:** Small victories can now lead to employees focusing on larger economies of scale challenges and initiatives that need to be achieved within the organization.

8. **Institute change:** During this final stage, senior leaders have to show their employees due to their due diligence and hard work the organization is exhibiting new successes. Ultimately, this newfound success will alter the behavior needed for this type of success to continue in the organization.

3.2 Five Methods Leaders Can Use to Shape and Cultivate Organizational Culture

Improving organizational culture is a long-term commitment that has to be the top priority for leaders to invest in. With the increased demands of the various stakeholders involved in the successful operations of organizations, leaders now must be flexible and transparent and continue to create more business opportunities for the growth of the internal and external environment. Leaders must align their organizational culture with their values, mission, and vision. The five methods or initiatives that leaders can implement to create a nurturing framework for their business and employees are as follows: develop a purposeful mission and vision, constantly evaluate existing culture, align leadership and communication, engage employees, and measure and forecast future benchmarks.

3.2.1 Developing a purposeful mission and vision

Organizations must shift their values, mission, and purpose to align with their employees' expectations. This can be done by developing an organizational culture that reflects how they support employees in reaching their maximum potential and creating a culture that uplifts and inspires employees to take calculated risks with repercussions from management. When employees firmly believe in an organization's purpose, mission, and vision they are more likely to be engaged and committed to the success of the organization. Externally organizations that exhibit a strong supportive organizational culture will be able to attract high-level employees to the company. This will ultimately lead to producing a more effective outcome.

3.2.2 Evaluating existing organizational culture

The second method that organizational leaders can implement to shape and cultivate organizational culture is continuously evaluating its existing culture. HR managers along with senior leaders need to develop functional metrics to identify areas of alarm inside the organization. Areas of concern that can be evaluated are absenteeism rate, sick time usage, and recruitment and retention. These metrics can identify negative corporate culture. This leads up to our third method where senior leaders need to align leadership and communication inside the internal environment.

3.2.3 Aligning leadership and communication

Senior leaders need to be authentic, open, and transparent in engaging with their employees. Initiate an open dialogue where both sides can build trust and develop a strong working relationship. Two-way communications create a unique partnership where both sides can experience acceptance, which will equal an improved organizational culture.

3.2.4 Engaging employees

The fourth method senior leaders need to implement internally to shape and cultivate organizational culture is engaging employees. Organizations that allow employees to be a part of their culture-planning activities will be able to gather information from various stakeholders' points of views. This will lead to a transformational shift of mindset from the employees' ability to model behavior that will be recognized with reaps of awards and benefits.

3.2.5 Measuring and planning for future benchmarks

The last method is being able to measure and plan for future benchmarks. Organizations must constantly measure their strides against their competitors and industry standards. Senior leaders must create processes where they will identify areas of opportunities and improvement internally. A strong culture is one that possesses employee stability and a consistent read on understanding how the marketplace trends and standings affect the survival rate of the company. Senior leaders who make organizational culture a top priority will be successful internally and externally.

The famous line, "culture eats strategy for breakfast" implies that culture is the main ingredient for creating learning opportunities and useful strategies. Senior leaders who understand that if the organizational strategy is not aligned with the organization's mission and vision, then employees will most likely be resisting change in the first place. A supportive and nurturing culture provides a safe space for learning and executing tasks necessary for profitability.

3.3 Recognizing Different Strategic Leadership Approaches to Drive DEI Structural Transformations

In order for organizations to drive DEI structural transformations, senior leaders have to structure their internal environments that value individuals from various economic and social perspectives. Such an environment is one that fosters innovation, creativity, and an increase in employee engagement that leads to increased productivity rates. Senior leaders must work with the HR Manager in embracing and promoting D&I initiatives at all levels of the organizational structure. A key initiative is forming diverse teams across the organization to solve problems and create opportunities to develop new innovative and creative products or services for customers. Stakeholders are more likely to support organizations whose final products are replicas of their target audience/customers. D&I initiatives assist organizations in building a loyal brand and customer base. Through alignment of goals, mission, and vision internally employees will be more committed in performing and producing above-average returns for their organization.

Building awareness is a key principle in driving DEI structural transformations through developing shared knowledge of the workforce's ability to become more proactive and engaged in establishing a DEI work environment. To build awareness senior leaders must financially and emotionally commit to introducing DEI language into policies, processes, and training in the internal environment. A DEI committee made up of various voices, and positions should be involved in the planning and implementation of these efforts inside the organization. The committee should solicit input from all the stakeholders to be able to secure a starting point to bring the DEI conversation to the executive table of the organization. This input will allow the HR manager to establish structure for developing metrics in tracking resources needed for employees success and structural transformation.

Structural transformation allows senior leaders to evaluate business processes across all departments within the organization. This will give an eye-opener approach to what obstacles or barriers are preventing the organization from creating an inclusive work environment. Here is an opportunity for each department to establish DEI goals and address the needs of every employee's ability to feel supported and engaged in their position with the company. Senior leaders will be able to collect this information and provide a report that shares the organization's progress with this initiative. A way to expand equal access to the report and establish transparency.

In 2014, Robin Ely and Davis A Thomas described the goal of diversity management at the macro level as one that involves organizations developing informal and formal relationships that affect the productivity rate and strategic outcomes. These authors indicated that three types of initiatives had to occur in the internal environment for diversity to be relevant at the organizational level. These three elements were: discrimination and fairness, access and legitimacy, and integration and learning. Ely and Thomas found that structural transformations were initiated inside the work environment when diverse teams operated under the integration and learning perspective. Integration and learning focuses on inter-group relations, and each group member feels that they are valued and respected by their colleagues. Through implementing integration strategies, organizations promote equal opportunity and a valuing culture where differences result in obtaining various perspectives which encourage open discussions in creating opportunities for successful business results. Finally, introducing integration and learning strategies helps secure trust throughout the organizational structure by recognizing employee differences as a unique opportunity to create innovative products and expand on building meaningful diverse relationships externally.

3.4 Implementing Emotional Intelligence Strategies to Embed DEI Policies and Processes Across Internal and External Environments

Emotional Intelligence is a concept that Daniel Goleman(2012) developed to assist an individual in examining one's emotions and how their emotions affect the work environment and relationships they can have with others. These emotions are seen as behavior attributes in how we engage and communicate with others around us. If organizational leaders can master emotional intelligence they can collaborate and utilize these newfound skill sets to empower others to share their ideas and opinions freely without falling into the pitfalls of groupthink.

Senior leaders who inquire about the mindset of emotional intelligence can create a safe and nurturing environment where they can inspire or motivate others to reach their maximum work potential. Emotional intelligence allows an individual, especially leaders to make impactful decisions during stressful work situations. Organizational leaders who can control their emotions are more likely to be effective in showing empathy and consideration for their employees' opinions. This approach will increase employee morale and internal engagement and will strengthen the relationship between employer and employee. Enhancing one's emotional intelligence is correlated to building meaningful relationships internally and externally. As well as developing social skills that can foster positive work environments and meaningful connections to their colleagues. Empowering one's ability to self-assess their impulse control can lead to more thoughtful and rational decisions and more emotional stability. This is a great pathway to be on for greater personal and professional development.

According to Goleman (1995), organizational leaders who possess an emotional Intelligence or emotional quotient (EQ) will enhance their ability to face change and unexpected challenges with resilience. Goleman believes that organizations that have leaders who exhibit emotional intelligence will have increased accountability in building trusting relationships, foster meaningful dialogues, become self-aware of their verbal and nonverbal language around others, and assist their employees in being grounded physically and mentally in and out of the organization.

When organizations embed emotional intelligence as part of their organizational framework they create synergy vibes that allow business-oriented solutions to be introduced through the introduction of diverse teams. These diverse teams can assist organizational leaders in identifying key principles, norms, and values to be inserted into current policies and processes. Emotional Intelligence can be a driving vehicle for networking and creating communication forums to share knowledge between departments for learning and growth opportunities. In other words, emotional intelligence sets perimeters for making difficult issues easier to discuss and develops benchmarks for employee and employer accountable behavior.

Figure 3.3   **Personal and social competence**

	Recognition	Regulation
Personal Competence	**Self-Awareness** • Self-confidence • Awareness of your emotional state • Recognizing how your behavior impacts others • Paying attention to how others influence your emotional state	**Self-Management** • Keeping disruptive emotions and impulses in check • Acting in congruence with your values • Handling change flexibly • Pursuing goals and opportunities despite obstacles and setbacks
Social Competence	**Social Awareness** • Picking up on the mood in the room • Caring what others are going through • Hearing what the other person is "really" saying	**Relationship Management** • Getting along well with others • Handling conflict effectively • Clearly expressing ideas/information • Using sensitivity to another person's feeling (empathy) to manage interactions successfully

Source: MSc, L. R. (2019, March 12). *Emotional intelligence frameworks, charts, diagrams & graphs.* PositivePsychology.Com. https://positivepsychology.com/emotional-intelligence-frameworks/

In 1995, Goleman delineated his model of emotional intelligence into five key areas: understanding one's own emotions, controlling one's emotions, self-motivation, recognizing and understanding others' emotions, and managing relationships. These areas formed the basis for Goleman's division of emotional intelligence into four quadrants: self-awareness, social awareness, self-management, and relationship management.

Figure 3.3 shown above is important in the realm of understanding the personal and social impact DEI has on us as individuals. As described in the figure, self-awareness is an important trait to develop. This trait allows leaders to understand how their emotions can impact the work environment in a positive or negative manner. Being cognizant of how they are communicating to others verbally and non-verbally. Social awareness entails how leaders inside the organization can make their employees feel more welcome and valued. Telling your employees you appreciate the time and effort they put in to complete a particular task or project is a part of social awareness. Being nice to people will go a long way in creating a harmonious work environment and increasing the productivity rate of that individual. The third trait is self-management. Self-management delves into an individual's mental and physical capabilities to monitor and control their actions and feelings. In other words, DEI leaders know how to leverage their emotions by controlling when they need to be expressed, and how to display various emotions to keep the conversation conducive to the situation at hand. Finally, relationship management is the ability of a leader to articulate their vision that promotes collaboration and teamwork. Leaders must focus on building relationships with their employees to be able to engage in difficult conversations that challenge their own perspectives. These conversations will lead to building a safe, collaborative space where various viewpoints can be challenged in a respectable way to get the best results.

3.5 Acknowledging the Requirement to Institutionalize DEI Transformations

For organizations to prepare for institutionalizing DEI transformations, they have to incorporate equity in daily operations and system processes. Senior leaders must examine if there are any social and economic inequalities that exist in their hiring practices, compensation, and leadership composition or make-up. By assessing these components senior leaders can determine if any discrimination or unconscious behavior is appearing in the internal work environment. If so, then clear goals, and objectives can be created to eliminate these behaviors and begin to develop D&I initiatives as a new foundation of fairness and equity.

Human resource managers will be at the forefront of creating these new D&I initiatives by communicating clear and concise expectations. In addition, provide DEI training and resources to managers and the Board of Governance to report and create DEI strategies for the organization. DEI strategies should include determining roles and responsibilities of who will be in charge of overseeing this mega effort. These strategies should allow for coordination of the DEI goals and objectives to measure effectiveness. Holding these individuals accountable for transparency and constant reports to the senior leaders for review. Once goals are established and defined, the human resource manager along with other key participants must determine how to correlate these new DEI initiatives with the mission and vision of the organization.

Kendi (2019) indicates that to have a complete buy-in mentality from senior leaders when initiating new DEI goals and objectives they must develop a guiding principle or diversity statement. These statements will provide a comprehensive roadmap that includes communication, guidance and thought processes of how the organization will move forward in its DEI efforts. This roadmap will prepare the organization to properly identify the needs of the stakeholders and collaborate with these groups in integrating key initiatives across every department of the organization.

To summarize this section, if organizations want to create a culture change and develop a bonding trusting relationship with their employees, action will need to be supported by SME (subject matter experts) in the organization who can provide resources for sustainability now and in the future. Organizational leaders will need to take a personal stake in this continuum change.

Chapter **4**

Building Blocks for Establishing Diversity, Equity, and Inclusion

In Chapter 4, we will identify the building blocks that will be imperative for organizational leaders to implement and lead DEI initiatives within the compounds of their internal workplace environment. These building blocks will be critical in cultivating a sense of belonging. Building blocks of creating a sense of community within an organization include: establishing affinity groups, attracting diverse talent; tackling gender pay differences; and DEI leadership development. This section will go into detail on how these elements are crucial in fostering a DEI working environment.

Key learning objectives include the reader's understanding of the following:

- Establishing affinity groups for enhanced internal networking and collaborative opportunities

- Attracting diverse talent and recruitment of minority employees and managers

- Recognizing DEI initiatives as a strategy to tackle gender pay discrepancies

- Linking Porter's five forces model with DEI leadership development

- Setting up a minority mentorship initiative as part of DEI cross-cultural programs

4.1 Forming Affinity Groups for Internal Networking and Collaboration Opportunities

Figure: 4.1   **Benefits of affinity groups**

The five business areas most affected by employee affinity groups are as follows:

1. Recruitment and Retention
2. Community Outreach
3. Professional Development
4. Human Resources Policy
5. Marketing to Employees

Source: Adapted from BoldBusiness.com; CTR Factor, Inc.

Figure 4.1 lists the five elements inside the organization that are affected by the formation groups: recruitment and retention; community outreach; professional development; human resource policies; and marketing to employees. Affinity groups affect recruitment and retention by attracting more diverse candidates to apply for internal vacancies. In addition, reduces the turnover rate and increases employee morale by allowing employees to be more engaged with their colleagues in a safe space to discuss potential solutions to issues that are affecting their mental and physical capacities. By having an affinity group, a sense of belonging can occur which leads to a community of acceptance and could play a vital role in the decision-making process of altering the internal work environment inside the organization. Professional development if it is part of the affinity group designed as a mentoring attribute can lead to shared knowledge. In order for monetary time and commitment to be geared towards the DEI movement inside the organization, human resource policies have to be developed and marketed by senior leaders. Finally, if affinity groups are marketed in the organization, they can be recognized through the organization's Intranet and by asking these groups to be a part of a committee where their work and ideas can be discussed to make a difference in connectivity with the decision-makers of the organization.

In addition to the positive career and personal outcomes for employees, to be effective within the organization affinity groups need support from the top brass. An affinity group is a group of individuals who connect in a work setting that is linked by a common interest or common goal. Affinity groups are a key element in enhancing an organization's DEI initiatives by creating a safe place where employees can cultivate a sense of community and belonging.

The affinity group will need to be geared towards matching the organization's vision, mission, and values to be relevant in receiving support from the top hierarchy decision-makers.

A successful affinity group formation must benefit the organization's structure in order to develop networking and collaboration opportunities with key leaders inside the organization. The benefits of affinity groups for the organization depend on achieving the following attributes: increased employee engagement, more women and minorities in leadership positions, and higher productivity outcomes.

For an affinity group to be effective, it also has to identify who are the key stakeholders inside the organizations who can work with them to bring key messages back to the senior leaders for an open dialogue to discuss opportunities and change efforts in policies and procedures. In other words, who are the champions inside the organization who can work with these groups to lead the change in reviewing DEI efforts? Clear expectations from both parties have to be clearly stated from the beginning to ensure transparency and to establish communication lines. During this time establishing perimeters of what each side needs from the other to be successful in this new joint venture.

It is imperative once the affinity group has been formed that they identify the process of recruiting members and narrowing down the focus or purpose of the group formation. Affinity groups are usually formed to establish a community with a certain group of employees who work within the compounds of the organization. Affinity groups can be formed based on religion, ethnicity, or common goals or purposes. For example; book clubs, social clubs, or associations. However, in the case of DEI revelations inside the organization, I am presenting the point that affinity groups should be focusing on fostering DEI training, promoting fairness and equity throughout each organizational department, and monitoring the progression of DEI initiatives being introduced into the organizational structure.

Figure 4.2   **Purposes of affinity groups**

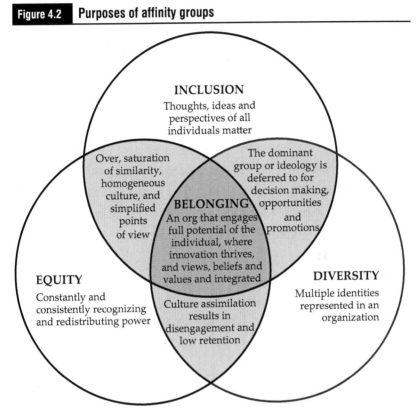

INCLUSION
Thoughts, ideas and
perspectives of all
individuals matter

Over, saturation
of similarity,
homogeneous
culture, and
simplified
points
of view

The dominant
group or ideology is
deferred to for
decision making,
opportunities
and
promotions

BELONGING
An org that engages
full potential of the
individual, where
innovation thrives,
and views, beliefs and
values and integrated

EQUITY
Constantly and
consistently recognizing
and redistributing power

Culture assimilation
results in
disengagement and
low retention

DIVERSITY
Multiple identities
represented in an
organization

Source: https://eventgarde.com

Based on Figure 4.2 above, affinity groups allow ideas and data formulation. These groups provide a safe place where different ideologies can be brought together to prioritize or develop common themes or similarities based on each member's experience with the organization. Creating a list of concepts aligned with the organization's mission and vision can bring a sense of belonging to the affinity group members. In turn, this will lead to a more conceptual focus that the senior leaders can identify as DEI initiatives to work on internally.

Beverly Daniel Tatum (2021) believed that affinity groups are designed to create nurturing supportive environments where all of its members can collectively add their voices in enhancing values of equality and participative decision-making into practice. These affinity groups provide a safe place where all voices can be heard, and a common decision can be made and then taken back to the decision-makers of the organization.

Autonomy and effectiveness are two attributes that can accurately describe the environment of an affinity group. These attributes allow the affinity group members to respond quickly in coming up with solutions to the designed problem the group has identified in the macro environment of the organization. Based on the affinity group members having a shared interest in tackling a particular problem in the overall structure of the organization it creates a sustainable and reliable way to plan execution of submitting these items to the decision-makers of the organization. This is where the champion identified in leadership will guide and support the affinity group in presenting these items to the key officials in the senior hierarchy.

Tulshyan (2016) described affinity groups and Employee Resource Groups (ERGs) as the most crucial elements of the building blocks in cultivating a culture of diversity and inclusivity within the internal work environment of any organization for competitive advantage. These groups help enhance or integrate the existence of self-awareness, and a sense of belonging for employees of marginalized communities who work inside the organization. Often affinity groups can begin to work with the top brass in creating internal resources such as mentorship programs and retention strategies to be integrated inside the organization.

Hekman (2015) firmly believed organizations should use affinity groups as an internal resource to educate senior leaders about biases and faulty processes that hinder the organization's effort to address diversity, equity, and inclusion. Senior leaders who want to establish unity and fairness must welcome this inclusive message and proceed to comprehensively focus on the attitudes and mindsets of those who have the power to reconstruct policies to support the transformations of the organizational structure internally and eventually externally. Affinity groups will assist senior leaders in responding correctly to resistance in addressing DEI Initiatives. These DEI Initiatives must be linked to the organization's mission, vision, and core competencies. Incentives must be attached to get resistors aboard to reach diversity goals. Affinity groups are the beginning of a journey that allows key leaders in the organization to examine its purpose in satisfying the needs of all of its stakeholders, starting with their employees.

4.2 Recruitment of Minority Employees and Managers

For organizations to be successful in attracting diverse talent they must have already cultivated a DEI company culture. Organizations can start by promoting diversity through their branding, developing their websites with employee-generated material, and showing diversity through images of various elements such as highlighting age differences, ethnicity, religious affiliations, and employee-generated content on the organization's website pages. Social media should be an outlet to display various activities that are occurring internally and externally that exhibit DEI practices and commitments from senior leaders.

Organizations have to be proactive in attracting diverse talent by adding historically black colleges and minority institutions to their employment pool databases when recruiting opportunities arise with the organization. Recruiting can be done by initiating an employee referral program. This employee referral program can give direct links to candidates from marginalized and underrepresented groups. HR managers should work continuously in updating and reconstructing job descriptions to be more inclusive. Equity statements should be included on job vacancies to encourage diverse applicants to apply. Another initiative is to conduct blind resume reviews. Blind resume reviews occur when non-essential information is removed prior to the hiring manager screening the application/resume. Non-essential information includes elements such as name, mailing address, and date when the applicant completed education. By initiating this activity unconscious bias can be curved and every applicant can have a level playing field of success of getting interviewed and perhaps hired.

Dubbin (2009) was highly animated when indicating HR managers had to take the lead in initiating diversity recruiting strategies in support of internal D&I hiring strategies. Diversity recruiting is crucial in enhancing unique perspectives of decision-making and offering holistic customer insight into more suitable products or services. DEI recruiting and hiring practices are an experiential and humanistic approach to developing a fair and equitable learning and workplace environment. Equitable hiring practices allow potential candidates and current employees an opportunity for success inside an organization. When your workforce resembles society this gives an organization a competitive edge and the capability to be creative and innovative in introducing new products and services to an untapped group of people. Basically, DEI is a building block for including all of your stakeholders' perspectives and gaining a high probability of increasing the organization's bottom line.

4.3 Acknowledging DEI Efforts as Means to Address Gender Pay Disparities

Addressing gender pay disparities and promoting DEI can improve overall employee morale and engagement. Making DEI efforts as an organizational goal will show employees their true value and the uniqueness they offer to the workplace. The first step in evaluating gender disparities in the workplace is to examine current pay metrics and pay policies in place. This internal examination of practices and pay policies should include entry-level pay, merit process, and compare and contrast salaries of men versus women. Examining the breakdown of this pay process involves looking at the average pay for marginalized employees in the organization, and comparing them to their counterparts in the same position within the organization. Promotions are also a great starting point to see who is moving up through the organization and what they are being compensated for. Increased pay equity can assist the HR department in attracting and retaining top talent and show transparency during this process. Monitoring promotions and various internal movements of marginalized groups will be a key driver in indicating where the organization has developed a successful promotion practice in their organization.

According to Sandberg (2013), the COO of Facebook, HR managers should periodically review their compensation packages to see if they are competitive and meet the industry standards. This review should include representation metrics where demographic data such as gender, race ethnicity, age, and disability is part of the analysis process. Pay equity is a critical element in evaluating an organization's commitment to fair and ethical compensation policies and practices. Senior leaders along with the HR department need to constantly measure elements such as retention rates. Retention rates can help identify specific information on groups that are leaving the organization. This would be a clear signal that there might be unconscious bias or lack of inclusion occurring in various departments within the organization.

Handling gender pay inequalities includes setting achievable target goals that begin with clearly having an understanding of the current workplace situation and developing a benchmark to compare against industry standards or nearest competitors. This benchmark is your SWOT analysis tool where organizational leaders can understand what goals they have achieved and the ones that still need improvement. HR can also work with organizational leaders to increase access to paid leave and childcare perks to enable women and marginalized employees to be more effective in their duties. More organizations since post-COVID-19 are offering alternative work schedules to assist in providing a work-life balance, which can assist women in saving more money and time in commuting back and forth to work. To bridge the gap of gender pay inequalities, organizations must strive to implement salary transparency and gender pay reporting. This collective action will contribute to a more equitable work environment where every employee can receive fair compensation and equal opportunities inside their workplace.

4.4 Connecting Porter's Five Forces Model to DEI Leadership Enhancement

Porter's five force model (1980) is crucial in allowing organizational leaders to see how DEI initiatives can enhance competitive advantage by determining its profitability level and the level of competition with their competitors. This strategy model allows organizational leaders to gather and disseminate information, analyze, and formulate these strategies so everyone inside the organization can understand the seriousness of how these five forces are detrimental to the success of the overall operations of the organization. Porter's five force model encourages senior leaders to be able to understand what strategy is required to stay competitive within the industry of the organization. These five forces which I will identify momentarily will allow these senior leaders opportunities to make more realistic decisions, identify areas of improvement, and increase their strengths and capacities to have a competitive edge in the industry marketplace.

| Figure 4.3 | Porter's five force model |

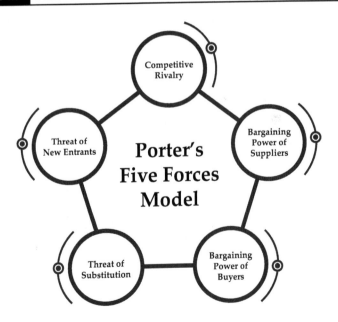

Source: *Porter's five forces: The ultimate competitive strategy blueprint.* (n.d.). Retrieved September 24, 2024, from https://www.thestrategyinstitute.org/insights/porters-five-forces-the-ultimate-competitive-strategy-blueprint

Porter's five-force model is broken down into five forces as shown in Figure 4.3. These forces include:

1. Competitive rivalry

2. Supplier power

3. Buyer power

4. Threat of substitution

5. Threat of new entry

In the next couple of paragraphs, I will define what each force consists of and how it relates to enhancing DEI leadership.

4.4.1 Competitive rivalry

The first force is called competitive rivalry, which is the organization's ability to survey who are your competitors and identify their strengths. In this particular force, leaders are comparing and contrasting their products, and services with their competitors. An organization that promotes DEI can achieve competitiveness by creating diverse teams that can bring out new ideas and perspectives which can bring different target customers to your organization, which can ultimately lead to enhanced customer satisfaction and increased market share. Organizations that can create a DEI image with the public eye can be viewed more favorably by their shareholders. These shareholders include customers, employees, investors, suppliers, and distributors. All of this is correlated to improving the organization's brand recognition and increasing profitability.

4.4.2 Supplier power

Porter's second force is called supplier power. In this force, suppliers gain the power to determine the price and the availability of resources and inputs to organizations. Organizations that want to gain a competitive edge over their competitors in being able to control resource scarcity can utilize businesses owned by minority-owned individuals. Resource scarcity occurs when there are limited resources and unlimited wants. Prices will increase when resources become scarce. When this happens, raw materials become harder to find. This becomes a tremendous opportunity for minority-owned businesses to become partners with these organizations to provide them with a high-quality substitute product to offer to their customers. Organizations using minority-owned businesses as a part of their supply-management chain can be a win-win solution for the organizations to still remain relevant in meeting the economic and social demands of society.

By using diversified suppliers, organizations can increase innovation, and empower competitiveness and socioeconomic awareness in diverse geographic areas and communities. When organizations develop supplier diversity they are more likely to see the increased effect of consumer spending and employee support.

4.4.3 Buyer power

The third force, called buyer power, refers to the scenario of customers putting pressure on businesses to provide higher quality products, offer better customer service, and offer lower prices. Buyer power in correlation to DEI allows senior leaders to reflect the needs of their diverse customer base by offering products that spark value in the minds of various marginalized groups. Organizations that perfect and understand this principle can become trailblazers in increasing their market share by providing a heavy influence on the consumer market. Values and beliefs are two attributes that can increase social awareness in consumer support. In order to be effective, organizations must align their industry position to understand and serve a diverse consumer market effectively.

4.4.4 Thread of substitution

The fourth force is labeled as a threat of substitution. This force is defined when your competitors can offer a more reliable product or service of higher quality, or offer the same items at a lower price. Consumers then have greater flexibility of choices in selecting what company they will choose to purchase their products or services from. In terms of DEI, an organization that can show value and display products and services that represent marginalized groups is more likely to be more successful in reeling these individuals into being a part of their organizations' dealings.

4.4.5 Threat of new entry

The last force in Porter's five force model is known as the threat of new entry. The threat of new entry is the organization's capability to enter into a new market to offer innovative and unique products or services to customers of that market. Also, it is deemed the risk a new organization creates for current organizations operating in that industry currently. What does this mean for DEI Leaders? DEI leaders can find a unique selling point targeted to marginalized groups to gain support in entering this new market. In addition, DEI can offer pricing strategies to attract various ethnic groups to their organizations' offerings of services and products. Finally, DEI organizations can partner with diverse community leaders and businesses to become significant partners or investors in entering new markets. This will provide public transparency that they are a fair and equitable organization to support.

4.5 Setting Up a Minority Mentorship Initiative as Part of DEI Cross-Cultural Programs

Figure 4.4 Cross-cultural competencies

Mindfulness   Mutuality   Inclusiveness   Creativity   Communication

Source: Adapted from https://multiculturalyou.com

As indicated in Figure 4.4, cross-cultural competency brings organizations the ability to provide awareness, acceptance, and respect to everyone who is involved with the success of the organization. When an organization has a clear understanding of their workforce and their employee culture, values, and beliefs they become the essence of workplace DEI initiatives. Cross-cultural programs enhance sensitivity towards cultural differences and are the building blocks of building communication dialogue between employer and employee. One of the key elements of cross-cultural programming is mentorship. Mentorship is a great way to integrate learning and engagement with employees who are at various levels of development and growth. This is an excellent initiative for marginalized groups working in organizations. Through mentorship programs marginalized groups will learn industry knowledge and develop key networking opportunities with the decision-makers inside the organization. Mentorship programs are a major step in career progression in the organization for women and other marginalized groups.

Mentoring programs are the structural foundations of organizations that are trying to create a DEI internal work environment. Not only do you provide the mentee an equitable opportunity for personal growth, but the mentor learns how to communicate and transfer crucial skill sets to another human being. A big part of DEI is inclusion and equity. Mentoring programs that are part of cross-cultural programs provide a powerful tool for cultural change and eradicating implicit bias and systemic racism. As you get to know someone on a personal one-on-one basis for an extended period of time, you can develop a different mindset and perspective of those who are different from themselves. Organizations that establish cross-culture programs such as mentorship initiatives send a clear message that they want to increase the representation of marginalized individuals at various levels within the organization.

Dr. Audrey J. Murrell (2009) who co-authored a book titled "Mentoring Diverse Leaders: Creating Change for People, Processes, and Paradigms" along with Stacy Blake-Beard and Diana Bilimoria argues that diversity mentoring was the best way for organizations to gain an edge over their industry competitor. The main focus of this book was to create a step-by-step guide in forming effective diverse mentorship programs for organizations. All of the authors involved in writing the book mentioned above indicated diverse mentorship programs are crucial in promoting DEI initiatives in the workplace because they lead to increased self-confidence and morale among employees and promote social equity in the organization. Dr. Murrell firmly believed that diversity mentoring programs help to identify new talent in the organization as well as create upskilling and upscaling with current employees.

The first step to creating a successful diversity mentorship program is understanding the goals and objectives of the program. All goals of the mentorship program should be aligned with the organization's mission and vision. This will help to get the buy-in of all of the senior executive team members and crucial decision-makers of the organization. The senior leadership team's involvement is crucial in helping recruit the right mentors for the program. These mentors will be trained to align the mentoring program with the business objectives and diversity goals of the organization. Senior leaders can work with the HR department in selection of the mentees who have an excellent performance benchmark based on their current and previous job evaluations. Cultural sensitivity training should be the core basis for designated mentors to take. The effect of this training will allow these mentors to be aware of issues and roadblocks that have hindered marginalized individuals from growing and developing. Furthermore, a diverse mentorship program should be engaging and interactive. The HR department should work with the mentors and create a template where all expected outcomes can be listed and reviewed bi-weekly to capture the mentees' progression. Resources should be made available if support is deemed necessary by either the mentor or mentee at any time during the duration of the mentorship program. To conclude, a well-thought-out and designed diversity training program can provide a high level of return on investment for both the organization and individual employees participating.

Chapter **5**

DEI Strategies for the Future

D EI strategies for the future lay the foundations for how organizations can be committed to enhancing diversity, equity, and inclusion in today's work environment. Senior leaders must create a learning and supportive atmosphere for everyone to be successful. To acquire this flourishing work environment, employees must feel valued and welcome. Policies and internal training have to be created to allow for a cultural shift of thinking, and resource allocation to everyone, not just designated groups inside the organization. Safe spaces must be incorporated especially for marginalized groups to be able to have a chance for professional and personal growth. In addition, senior leaders must assist the HR department in establishing clear and concise performance metrics and creating a DEI Interview and hiring committee to have an immediate impact in recruiting diverse talents into the organization. Finally, create a formal and informal networking opportunity to assist everyone in maximizing their work potential skill sets.

Chapter 5 will examine key developments that must occur inside organizations to meet the challenges and demands of creating DEI working environments for the future. Flexibility and intersectionality will be essential for senior leaders to prioritize sustainable practices and corporate social responsibility. A new commitment from leadership and strategic planning has to be the core DEI strategic plan to include detailed actions that need to be executed in the daily standard operating procedures. Chapter 5 will consist of the following elements listed below:

Key learning objectives include the reader's understanding of the following:

- Cultivating a sustainable culture for a DEI mindset

- Measuring DEI criteria for strategic development

- Establishing DEI processes in the workplace

- Understanding role assessment and role definition

- Developing contingency plans for DEI strategies

5.1 Cultivating a Sustainable Culture for a DEI Mindset

Figure 5.1 entails the nature of cultivating an inclusive DEI mindset. This mindset is how we as individuals engage and interact with others around us. Being able to enhance our understanding of learning how to embrace and work with others who possess differences in viewpoints, values, and cultural journeys. Organization leaders will be tasked with developing a working environment where freedom to express individual uniqueness is celebrated and supported. This uniqueness will assist the organization in bringing solutions and innovations to product development and building a stronger customer relationship. Senior leaders must build a DEI environment where shared knowledge, learning, and transparency can occur. Shared learning is a vital component for an organization to build a competitive advantage over industry competitors, by enhancing decision-making opportunities and providing freedom for every employee to be an active player in the success of the organization's ROI (Return on Investment).

| Figure 5.1 | **Inclusive DEI mindset components** |

Source: Adapted from https://miro.medium.com

Developing a sustainable inclusive mindset involves allowing both the employer and employee the opportunity to engage in respectful communication dialogues. Through this dialogue, self-reflection and self-evaluation can occur in learning how successful each person is in confronting their own social and unconscious biases. Only when this happens can an organization truly move toward connection and personal growth by embracing DEI initiatives inside the organization. Organizations will need to incorporate policies and processes to bring inclusivity and diversity to the forefront of the new workforce development. Continuing movement and constant practice will create an opportunity for a positive change in the mindset of those who are working in this enhanced DEI internal environment.

5.1.1 Ecological intelligence and DEI

Figure 5.2   **Ecological intelligence model by Daniel Goleman**

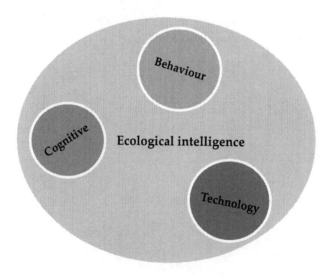

Source: Adapted from https://www.researchgate.net

Figure 5.2 displays the three elements of ecological intelligence by Goleman (1995). The first element of ecological intelligence is cognition. Cognition is the ability to feel like you are connected to everything in your presence. For an employee to have a sense of belonging, they must be able to understand their interactions with their environment. One's perception and representation of being valued is the key to eliminating barriers and boundaries of systemic racism in organizations. The second element of ecological intelligence is behavior. Our behavior dictates how we are going to maneuver and work within the compounds of the rules and regulations of the organization. An employee's behavior can be a critical factor in how they learn and are able to implement this new knowledge in the work environment. Technology is the final element of ecological intelligence. This element provides the pathway in which employees and employers communicate with each other and their customer base. Technology allows data sharing and collaboration throughout the entire organization to be able to make crucial decisions that affect the direction and strategies to be implemented for organizational success.

Daniel Goleman (2009), in his book "Ecological Intelligence: How Knowing the Hidden Impacts of What We Buy Can Change Everything" indicated ecological footprint analysis has to be used to quantify the environmental impact of a product or activity in terms of the resources consumed and waste generated. Daniel Goleman believed that ecological intelligence allowed us as individuals to understand the complexity of the systems around us. In other words, employees need their colleagues and employers to assist them navigate around their work environment successfully. Collaboration and our social intelligence to survive any challenges that arise in our environment. Shared intelligence allows us the opportunity to have advanced understanding to master our daily tasks and gain knowledge to exchange information that is important in our existence to our current environment expectations. As employees in our ecological work environment, we need to know our impact, favor our improvements, and share what we learn to increase continuous improvement within the organization's social structure.

5.2 Measuring DEI Criteria for Strategic Development

Figure 5.3	14 HR metrics for measuring DEI

Source: Adapted from: https://www.aihr.com

For a business to continue to evolve and gain a competitive advantage over its competitors, strategic planning has to reflect the organization's workplace culture. Therefore, understanding diversity, equity, and inclusion is essential in measuring the success or failure of an organization's ability to address its connection to its employees. Figure 5.3 provides 14 HR metrics examples that HR managers along with senior leadership can use to measure the effectiveness of implementing DEI initiatives inside the organization. Some of these metrics can be incorporated by looking at the socio/economic status, age, gender, race, disability, job titles, gender pay differences, and longevity rate of the employees. These dimensions help paint a comprehensive picture of the areas inside the organization where improvements need to be addressed.

Hiring practices such as looking at the dimensions of the organization's applicant pool can give the organization leaders a sense of the breakdown of workforce representation. Representation allows your organization to provide a fair and equitable playing field for individuals of all backgrounds to be a part of the workforce composition. Senior leaders also need to delve into reviewing employee turnover and attrition and see if it is correlated to the workplace representation within the organization. Remember, even if an organization is diverse, it doesn't mean that it is this way at every level of the organization. Especially, at the top level where decisions are being made. Furthermore, HR managers need to take into account metrics such as access to professional development and mentorship. These factors can assist the organization in determining how they are actively supporting their employees in thriving professionally and personally. Accessibility is a key component in making sure senior leaders are creating a safe place and employees are being supported by the organizational structure in place. DEI has to be aligned with the strategic planning phase of the organization. By initiating this concept, DEI becomes interconnected with the mission, values, and core competencies of the organization. For an organization to be successful and thorough in measuring its DEI benchmarks you only need to look at how much money is being allocated to this area.

Deloitte(2022 DEI Transparency Report, n.d.) indicated for metrics to be meaningful to organizations they need to focus on measuring the organizational structure then the individual. In other words, establishing a corporate culture where biases will not be tolerated will ultimately affect the behavior and accountability of the employee's ability to improve the equitable outcomes desired. In addition, organizations must frequently collect and analyze employee data to provide key insight into what direction the organization is going as far as meeting its DEI benchmarks. Finally, Deloitte (2022 DEI Transparency Report, n.d.) firmly believes that organizations that include DEI metrics as part of their strategic planning will be able to correlate this with their business objectives which will lead to a more comprehensive competitive advantage in market valuation and operational efficiency. DEI outcomes should be congruent with an organization's business outcomes. Therefore, providing the organization with an opportunity to lead an internal systemic change in achieving increased profitability or productivity.

5.3 Establishing DEI Processes in the Workplace

To establish DEI processes in the workplace organizational leaders have to understand the challenges and frustrations faced by the various marginalized groups and other employees working in the organization. In order to create engagement and ensure actionable results, a task force or DEI council should be initiated. A senior executive and employees from different levels of the organization should make up the members of the DEI council. This council's first call of action must be to develop short and long-term goals to be achieved. In addition, meeting cadence should be established such as how often will the council meet, where will the meeting take place, and clear collaboration and communication expectations for each member of the group.

A referral program should be created to recruit new members to join the DEI council so that new ideas and suggestions can be brought to the forefront of discussion. Furthermore, the DEI council should be involved in examining the hiring practices of the organization to make sure diversity is included in the advertising and selection of qualified applicants. Also, this council should work with the HR department in developing social activities for employees to celebrate multicultural events that are correlated to the various ethnic groups identified in the organization. Finally, the DEI council can create quarterly in-person or virtual roundtable discussions where DEI conversations can be held in a supported safe space. By initiating roundtable discussions this will allow the organization to begin the process of building trust and transparency with its employees.

Another key way to establish DEI processes in the workplace is to have the HR manager along with the senior executives of the organization develop a DEI vision and mission statement. To be effective this DEI statement has to be aligned with the strategic plan of the organization so it will not be a separate entity of the organization's DNA. This DEI statement should be clear, and concise on how the organization will conduct its daily standard of operation procedures in a more fair, and inclusive way. These two processes I describe will not be successful if senior executives do not exhibit leadership commitment. Which means resource allocations, accountability, and transparency from all levels of management in the organization.

One of the best ways to establish DEI processes in the workplace is to integrate the new DEI perspective into the marketing strategy, product development, and customer service framework to achieve increased profitability outcomes and innovation capabilities. DEI initiatives should be a part of any marketing campaign whether it is in print, social media, or website content. Initiating this step will allow the organization to enrich its message with authenticity and depth and incorporate more ethnicity to garner toward its products or services. If a company wants to gain a competitive advantage over their competitors DEI processes must be integrated into their product development. Creating internally diverse teams can ensure that specifications will meet the needs of their various customers' expectations. Finally, organizations can establish DEI processes by providing impactful internal training that is culturally sensitive in enabling employees to learn how to deal with customers from various backgrounds. HR is the department inside the organization that is the responsible party for mandating a work environment that is filled with inclusivity and initiates policies in setting accountability through current policies that address providing high-quality customer service to each and everyone that comes through the doors employees come in contact with.

According to Ferdman & Deane (2013), when organizations encourage the principles of inclusion to occur within the organization it becomes a collective behavior that leads to employees experiencing connectivity with their coworkers and employer. This new experience will be present in the attitudes, values, and norms associated with the new organizational and social context of the work environment.

5.4 Role Assessment and Role Evaluation

For this section, I will break down why role assessment and role evaluation are crucial in changing the mindset of organizations' decision-makers about the effect DEI has in creating a more productive and efficient environment. Let's begin to first define what role assessment and role evaluation really mean. Role assessment is defined as a critical tool to evaluate how employees are evaluated by the skill sets and mental capacities to actively perform their duties within the organization. These competencies are crucial in helping employees be able to improve their personal development for potential promotion and opportunities to seek higher-level positions in the organization. Role evaluation is the process that senior executives and the HR manager do on an annual basis to review existing jobs in the organization to see if these jobs still bring value to the organization. If these jobs do not bring value, then these designated jobs are restructured to be aligned with the needs of the organization. In addition, job evaluation ensures that the organization is offering competitive salaries and that the performance standards are appropriate to each position in the organization.

Role assessments and role evaluations are a critical roadmap for DEI initiatives to be a part of the strategic planning of an organization. Especially when it comes to the marginalized groups. Organization executives will need to focus on their capabilities of identifying potential employees for future leadership roles. This action will be able to provide employees with a realistic view of what skill sets they will need to acquire to excel in their roles. Role assessment and role evaluation will be able to assist the underrepresented employees in determining their own skill competency level. Organizational success in fostering a DEI work environment will heavily depend on creating a support lifeline to prepare marginalized employees for sustainable roles within the organization. Ultimately, this approach will allow the HR manager to create a succession and talent management plan to assist the organization's workforce, especially minorities in being matched to the right position in the organization.

Dr. Thomas DiTomaso (2013), believes that role assessment, especially role evaluation is the fundamental way to provide marginalized employees an opportunity to provide crucial feedback to assist organizational leaders in creating data to improve performance evaluation as well as create a high-quality outcome for meeting performance standards. Organizations that provide role assessment and role evaluation say to all of their employees they matter and we are committed to a comprehensive approach in assessing the needs throughout all levels.

5.5 Developing Contingency Plans for DEI Workplace Strategies

| Figure 5.4 | Contingency plan in 5 steps |

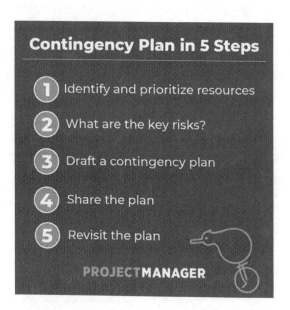

Source: Adapted from ProjectManager

Figure 5.4 displays the five steps that organizational leaders need to partake in to develop a contingency plan. The first step is identifying and prioritizing resources that help obtain the commitments of the organization executives in understanding how DEI initiatives create employees' well-being and job satisfaction. When employees have greater job satisfaction their productivity rate increases which relates to the overall success of the business's daily operations. Based on Glassdoor's 2019 Diversity and Inclusion Survey, 42% of U.S. employees indicated that they were victims or that they witnessed their coworkers suffer workplace discrimination. In addition, the survey also found that organizations that fostered inclusivity and provided professional growth development outperformed their competitors by 36%. By identifying and prioritizing resources organizations can help attract top talent which will eventually boost profits. Leadership commitment and developing new internal policies and processes are part of this contingency plan.

The second step in developing a contingency plan for DEI strategies is finding out what are the key risks. Lack of awareness is a key risk for DEI strategies implementation. Employee Surveys and education are key attributes that need to be done in order to understand how unconscious bias and prejudice can prevent the organization from achieving ROI. Open communications and dialogue initiated by the HR Manager can create a safe place where biases can be discussed and solutions can be discovered. Drafting A DEI Contingency plan is the third step where executives along with a DEI Committee can assist all departments inside the organization in creating action steps on how their department will address diversity issues. This includes detailing specific strategies for increasing and retaining underrepresented groups. In addition, as part of these strategies will be to frequently review and assess these strategies for effectiveness. Additionally, all senior executives should be required to take sensitive cultural training and anti-racist training. Furthermore, implement policies that will be included in the employee handbooks that promote equitable outcomes in all areas and aspects of the overall business operations. Encourage and facilitate the use of diversity and inclusivity in marketing strategies. Finally, to develop and implement a comprehensive system of accountability and assessment around DEI initiatives through hiring practices, promotion, and interaction with minority suppliers.

The fourth step of developing a contingency plan for DEI workplace strategies is sharing the plan. Initially, executive leaders should have an open dialogue where employees are free to ask questions and be given a copy of the plan for personal copy to review. HR managers should also speak of the significance of how this enhances and impacts the company internally and externally. Revisiting the plan is the final step in the contingency plan. During this step, the contingency plan should be reviewed and assessed on an annual basis. Senior executives will need to identify any new changes that affect the internal and external environments. This includes risk identification and seeing if the contingency plan is still aligned with the organization's business objectives. Also, make sure the contingency plan is aligned with meeting all of the needs of the stakeholders. To conclude a DEI contingency plan should improve assessment, and provide a clear insight into all areas of the organization. In addition, the contingency DEI plan should give the organization's employees and external stakeholders a clear direction to follow. Ultimately, contingency planning is a critical step in making sure the organization is relevant in satisfying its stakeholders' investment in the company's reputation and commitment to success.

Chapter 6

DEI Planning Tools

This chapter introduces a couple of DEI planning tools such as SWOT analysis and environmental scan. When properly utilized, these tools can reveal a lot about the level of DEI implementation within an organization and give decision-makers the opportunity to use the discovered leverage points to overcome DEI challenges by establishing DEI roles and responsibilities and collaborating or partnering with minority suppliers.

Key learning objectives should include the reader's understanding of the following:

- Defining SWOT analysis

- Introducing the environmental scan - Building buy-in from key stakeholders

- Understanding leverage points and challenges

- Establishing roles, responsibilities, and decision-making channels

- Developing partnerships with minority suppliers and distributors to lower customer engagement threats

6.1 Defining SWOT Analysis

The acronym SWOT stands for strengths, weaknesses, opportunities, and threats. In principle, SWOT analysis, as a crucial DEI planning tool, helps organizations identify their strengths, weaknesses, opportunities, and threats in relation to how they are currently managing diversity, equity, and inclusion (DEI) procedures in all areas of their day-to-day business processes. Figure 6.1 demonstrates what a DEI-focused SWOT analysis would look like.

Table 6.1   A DEI-focused SWOT analysis

Strengths	Weaknesses
• The organization has a culturally diverse workforce. • The organization's management slightly encourages the adoption of DEI initiatives. • The working environment is convenient for and accessible to all employees, irrespective of their demographics. • Good public reputation for exhibiting some DEI attributes.	• Lack of adequate recruitment or promotion of ethnic minorities and women. • Acute employee dissatisfaction with the current organizational policies, culture, and management style that are unfair and gender-based. • No clear and mandatory DEI policies. • Customers' dissatisfaction with the organization's lack of all-encompassing DEI implementation.

Opportunities	Threats
• Attraction of culturally diverse talent • Improving engagement scores among the staff • Lowering customer engagement threats • Highly productive and cohesive organization	• Unwillingness to expand the scope of the existing DEI programs • Limited budget and resources to maintain the current DEI policies • Having board members that aren't wholly motivated by DEI compliances. • Failure to train managers and supervisors about DEI requirements

As indicated in Table 6.1, in addition to having its reputation on the line, an organization that fails to initiate, promote, and maintain DEI policies has a lot to lose. Apart from dealing internally with a group of disgruntled employees, it will also have to confront dissatisfied customers who may be dismayed about its monolithic culture that is devoid of true DEI ideals.

6.2 Introducing the Environmental Scan - Building Buy-In from Key Stakeholders

Conducting a Diversity, Equity, and Inclusion (DEI) environmental scan is the first step every organization that aspires to initiate DEI policies into its processes or revamp its existing ones needs to take. This involves taking stock of its current DEI practices, creating a roadmap for the larger application of DEI principles, and formulating procedures for maintaining DEI initiatives.

To undertake a useful SWOT Analysis, an organization needs input from different key stakeholders that are directly connected to the organization's day-to-day operations. There are four intrinsic criteria that an organization usually wants to investigate so as to determine if its existing DEI procedures are working as envisaged or if they have flatly collapsed. These include:

1. **Understanding the "as-is" circumstances:** There are some questions that may be begging for immediate and factual answers when investigating the "as-is" DEI situations within an organization. Are all employees treated fairly and fully respected irrespective of their ethnicity, gender, religion, etc.? Does the organization put in place legally binding guidelines for encouraging DEI practices? Are customers currently happy with the organization's reputation as far as their DEI principles are concerned?

2. **Discovering the strategic gaps and areas requiring significant attention:** The true picture of DEI activities in an organization can be unearthed by simply obtaining correct responses to the above-mentioned questions. Some of the gaps that may be identified can include unfair recruiting and promotion practices, a gender-based pay system, the exclusion of minorities from senior management positions, or a total lack of DEI policies. As a matter of fact, those critical areas deserve swift and serious attention.

3. **Determining the organization's current strengths and capabilities:** After identifying the organization's strengths and capabilities through a well-structured SWOT Analysis, it is now time to tap into those strengths and make use of them to timely advance DEI policies in the organization under question.

4. **Establishing a realistic DEI model or program:** The first three criteria are helpful and instrumental in establishing a sustainable DEI model or program in any organization if properly executed.

An overarching environment scan can be undertaken by collecting useful information or data from both internal and external stakeholders. In order to have a balanced outcome from the scan, this may involve interviewing company leaders or executives, department managers, employees, and other internal stakeholders as well as obtaining input from customers, partners, investors, suppliers, creditors, governmental agencies, etc. Large corporations may resort to accessing public data from independently published publications, like journals, newspapers, government gazettes, and so on. Generally, surveys and questionnaires are the most readily used tools for carrying out DEI environmental scans.

While it is usually advisable that organizations explore building buy-ins from key stakeholders, efforts must be deployed towards passing the expressed, different opinions through the lens of DEI scrutiny. The main reason why many organizations have been struggling with the establishment and/or sustenance of their DEI initiatives is that the opponents of DEI are more powerful and continue to suppress the voices of those who are directly affected by the apparent lack of DEI practices within those organizations. Saxena (2014) expressed that "No two humans are alike. People are different in not only gender, culture, race, social and psychological characteristics but also in their perspectives and prejudices. Society has discriminated on these aspects for centuries." So, what opinions should be taken into consideration when stakeholders are deliberating on possible DEI policies or programs to implement within their organizations?

- **Valuable and considerate opinions:** The most important value any organization can exhibit is to hold genuine respect for the human rights of those working for it. Every country, including the United States, has laws that forbid discrimination of workers based on their religion, age, gender, political affiliation, etc. On June 21, 2021, President Biden issued an Executive Order on Diversity, Equity, Inclusion, and Accessibility in the Federal Workforce, urging all departments to remove any bottlenecks that might have been preventing minorities from having access or enjoying working in the Federal workforce.

- **Making sacrifices:** For DEI initiatives to be successfully introduced into any organization, sacrifices have to be made, from the executive level to the lowest-ranked employees. It is common for senior staff in some organizations to strongly oppose full DEI implementation because of the fear of losing some of their special privileges. Against this backdrop, Gotsis and Grimani (2016) believed that the character of servant leadership is one of the criteria for fostering inclusiveness in an organization.

6.3 Understanding Leverage Points and Challenges

Considering the DEI SWOT Analysis in Figure 6.1, it is apparent that organizations have some intrinsic strengths they can leverage against the mounting challenges that may threaten their organizational opportunities. In reality, different organizations are at different levels of their DEI implementations. In other words, the situations differ from one organization to the other. While some organizations have tremendously achieved full DEI implementation, others might embrace limited-version of DEI initiatives, and some organizations might have inexistent DEI approaches.

Referring to Figure 6.1. again, the following attributes can be regarded as leverage points that an organization can utilize to its advantage in order to jump-start an all-encompassing DEI implementation:

1. **Having a culturally diverse workforce:** As far as implementing DEI procedures, a culturally diverse organization is a shoulder above those that only practice monoethnic recruiting (hiring only from a single race). Having employees from different races who are cohesively working together indicates that there is some measure of DEI policies already in place in such a polyethnic organization (an organization that hires workers from different ethnicities). It won't be a major hassle for a polyethnic organization to fully adopt DEI initiatives because it has already put itself on that path with its interracial hiring practice, whether such a step was taken intentionally or not.

2. **Involvement of an organization's management in DEI initiatives:** When an organization's management is fully involved in DEI processes, a number of its executives will consequently turn themselves into champions of DEI ideology. They will not shy away from publicly promoting DEI programs aimed at creating homogeneity among their workforce.

3. **Convenient and accessible working environment:** In EY's 2023 "Belonging Barometer", which asked employed adults about their experiences with DEI, 75% of respondents expressed the disappointment of being excluded at work due to lack of flexibility on their organizations' part. They stated that they felt a sense of belonging when they could freely interact with colleagues at work. Not surprisingly, 63% of respondents from different generations currently appreciate working for organizations that have DEI policies in place, these included Gen Z and millennials.

4. **Good public reputation for DEI attributes:** Multinationals are considered staunch promoters of DEI programs because they have employees that cut across all nationalities, races, genders, etc. This is a structural strength that multinationals often utilize to command a good and admirable public reputation.

Despite the above-mentioned strengths or leverage points, an organization may still contend with some challenges arising from poor DEI implementation, such as the constant internal strife and hostility that are usually responsible for a negative working environment, high turnover as unhappy employees depart from toxic organizational culture, and lack of diversity in decision-making.

6.4 Establishing Roles, Responsibility, and Decision-making Channels

For any organization to make sensible progress in its DEI program so as to overcome some of the challenges confronting its workforce, clear roles, responsibilities, and decision-making channels must be established.

Some of the most common DEI roles and their corresponding responsibilities include:

1. **Equality, diversity, and inclusion (DEI) advisor:** A DEI advisor can be quite instrumental in helping an organization streamline its DEI initiatives. Advisors generally undertake environmental scans of the organization they are working for to evaluate and measure the success of their diversity approaches. They periodically conduct DEI seminars, and workshops, and lead diversity programs. In circumstances where the organizations' DEI initiatives are subpar or nonexistent, a DEI advisor will endeavor to introduce the best practices in the DEI concept to the organizations that hire them. Sometimes a DEI advisor may also be referred to as a DEI consultant or DEI specialist. DEI consultants have been properly licensed to do their jobs, and they may work part-time or full-time in an organization or attend simultaneously to different organizations' DEI requirements.

2. **Equality, diversity, and inclusion (DEI) manager:** Most DEI managers are in-house staff, that is, they solely work for an organization as an employee. Their duties are far more complex than those carried out by DEI specialists. Typically, DEI managers design and execute all-encompassing DEI strategies, concepts, and action plans in accordance with their organizations' values and business objectives. They also liaise with HR, management, and various departments to implement DEI principles into routine processes such as recruitment, hiring, training,

onboarding, and career development. By establishing and maintaining metrics, DEI managers measure the efficiency of their organizations' DEI programs and practices and make data-driven decisions as necessary. They regularly organize training, seminars, and workshops to instill DEI ideals in their organizations' workforce. Similarly, they interact with external organizations and communities to achieve partnerships in furthering DEI principles in the communities where they are operating. They quickly investigate and address any instances of occupational bias, harassment, or discrimination, creating a fair and inclusive environment for all employees by applying their knowledge of their industry's best DEI practices and trends.

3. **Head of equality, diversity, and inclusion:** This is more of an executive position, and a head of equality oversees the entire DEI department activities. A DEI manager reports directly to the head of equality.

4. **Director of equality, diversity, and inclusion:** A director of equality manages all the different departments under the DEI division. An organization's DEI division may contain other departments such as HR, research, legal, administrative, etc.

Figure 6.1 The DEI decision-making process in an organization

Figure 6.1 reveals how the DEI decision-making process works in an organization. The DEI policies are approved at the divisional level and passed down the hierarchy for implementation. DEI advisors or consultants, at the grassroot level, interact with employees to ensure that they comprehensively understand their organization's DEI principles and, in return, communicate their findings or observations to equity managers who escalate the information to the head of equity.

6.5 Building an Effective DEI Communication Strategy

To advance any program or principles within an organization, regular and effective communication is vital. The same applies to promoting DEI initiatives and policies. Building a DEI communication strategy requires three essential steps:

1. **Understanding your audience:** It is important to know who your employees are. What values do they hold dear, and what kind of DEI programs will excite or resonate with them? Even in DEI practices, there are no one-size-fits-all approaches. Most successful DEI programs succeed because they find acceptance with the targeted audience or employees. One main reason why DEI initiatives fail is that the target audience doesn't actually feel that the DEI policies or principles in place are helpful enough to prevent them from workplace harassment or maltreatment.

2. **Creating a clear DEI message:** It is equally advisable to create DEI messages that are clear and understandable to employees. Misleading or confusing communication is technically worse than no communication at all. When employees are confused, they are likely to misconstrue the DEI content and underrate their organization's good intentions. It is helpful to provide useful instructional materials, educational manuals, videos, and other resources that can help employees fully grasp what they stand to gain from their organization's DEI policies.

3. **Choosing appropriate communication channels:** When communicating DEI ideals to employees, it is sensible to use their preferred channels of communication. Some may prefer email, intranet chat, or reading the company's newsletter while others may react better to information passed across during a seminar or workshop. It is also important that there should be a regular or consistent exchange of useful information between DEI management and the employees.

6.6 Developing Partnerships with Minority Suppliers and Distributors to Lower Customer Engagement Threats

One of the serious threats an organization lacking a well-coordinated DEI could face, as shown in Table 6.1 is the customer engagement threat.

The old saying that people buy from an organization they like still stands true today. The United States, for example, has different ethnicities/races touting substantial buying power, as indicated in Table 6.2 below.

Table 6.2 **U.S. buying power by race/ethnicity, 2000-2023.**

US Buying Power*, by Race/Ethnicity, 2000-2023 billions				
	2000	2010	2018	2023
white	$6,413.3	$9,431.4	$12,147.7	$13,897.0
Black	$609.1	$961.2	$1,300.2	$1,533.1
Asian	$276.4	$603.5	$1,013.3	$1,333.1
Multiracial	$60.3	$143.1	$224.7	$295.3
Native American	$40.3	$82.5	$114.6	$136.4
Total	$7,399.4	$11,221.6	$14,800.6	$17,194.8
—Hispanic**	$494.0	$1,018.0	$1.539.0	$1,924.0

Note: numbers may not add up to total due to rounding; *defined as disposable personal income, meaning the share of total personal income available for personal consumption, personal interest payments and savings; ** "Hispanic" is an ethnicity rather than a race, and Hispanics can be of my race; racial group figures add up to total, while a separate breakout for non-Hispanics is not shown

Source: Selig Center for Economic Growth, Terry College of Business at the University of Georgia, "The Multicultural Economy 2018," March 21, 1019 https://www.emarketer.com

It is simple logic that any monoethnic organization that hires only from one race will have a hard time convincing buyers from other races or ethnicities to patronize its products/ services, except it is a necessity. Hence, one of the most probable approaches for lowering customer engagement threats is to partner with minority suppliers and distributors. With an enormous buying power estimated at over $1.5 trillion dollars, African Americans have a significant buying influence. For organizations to court their patronage, they should readily partner with African-American local suppliers and distributors so as to be able to maintain their market share. Failure to embrace African-American local suppliers will cause those organizations to lose a substantial segment of consumers that could have been loyal to their brands.

This page is intentionally left blank

Chapter 7

Foundation for Crafting a Robust Organizational DEI Strategy

In this chapter, efforts are made to describe the significance of conducting an organization-wide formative evaluation and how the outcomes of the evaluation can be used to establish DEI-compliant vision and language, formulate "SMART" objectives, establish accountability metrics, and actively promote diversity, equity, and inclusion within that organization.

Key learning objectives should include the reader's understanding of the following:

- Formative evaluation

- Establishing vision and organizational language.

- Formulating "SMART" objectives

- Establishing accountability metrics
- Learning how to promote openness and clarity

7.1 Formative Evaluation

In this age where all organizations want to be perceived publicly as fair and culturally diverse, sometimes showing a deceptive tendency by including people of different races in their advertising, it takes a comprehensive formative evaluation to discover how deep they are in embracing DEI ideals. Enders et al. (2021) recognized that the primary objective for undertaking a comprehensive DEI formative evaluation is to assess an organization's and its management's perceptions toward a planned DEI initiative and discover what subgroups within the organization's professional hierarchy are doing in support of or against the full implementation of DEI ideals.

This entails that there wouldn't be the slightest chance to build inclusion and mitigate the impacts of sexism, racism, and systemic biases if efforts are not deployed toward evaluating the organization's DEI propensities.

As a sensitive step in pre-DEI implementation, undertaking a formative evaluation for DEI purposes requires taking certain, ethical criteria into consideration, such as ensuring that the organization-wide assessment is:

1. **Equity-focused:** When planning a company-wide evaluation, it is imperative to pay serious attention to fostering balanced equity when it comes to selecting team members to carry out the evaluation. The most sensible way to ensure diversity in

the evaluation team members is to include stakeholders from all demographics, if possible. This entails that there should be representatives of different genders, races, ethnicities, skills, ranks and files, levels of expertise, experience, and knowledge among the evaluation team. It makes sense to include people from the group that is being evaluated. Otherwise, if all the evaluation team members are chosen from a single ethnicity or from only among the senior management or C-suite, a narrow population, the outcome of the evaluation will be lopsided and unreliable.

2. **Culturally considerate:** In addition to an overarching organizational culture, most companies in America have some subcultures, irrespective of their sizes—whether they are small, medium, or large enterprises. These subcultures, albeit unofficial, are what cement relationships among employees who share similar traits or characteristics. It is not rare at all to identify ethnic, religious, gender, social, and academic subcultures inside an organization. It simply means people from the same ethnicity or who embrace similar religions tend to cling together at the workplace, and this apparent bond makes them feel included in their working environment. Therefore, when choosing an evaluation team, efforts must be deployed toward recognizing the existing subcultures and making sure that they are properly represented.

3. **Across-board participation:** While it is not feasible for all employees to join the evaluation team, their opinions and ideas can be collected via surveys, questionnaires, departmental meetings, and contributions to internal messaging newsletters or intranet, where employees are encouraged to voice their opinions about certain aspects of their working experiences they found unsatisfactory.

Undoubtedly, this approach promotes across-board participation in the assessment process. As a matter of fact, there wouldn't be a fair and inclusive initiative if everyone's concerns and aspirations weren't considered and recognized in the course of the evaluation.

7.1.1 Steps for achieving a successful formative DEI evaluation

There are some logical steps an organization is expected to follow if it aspires to conduct its DEI assessment successfully. They include:

1. **Using fair and respectful context:** The texts, images, questions, illustrations, and language used to draw the evaluation context should not undermine the integrity and honor of all the communities within the organization. Utilizing offensive language or discriminatory images may cause those slighted subcultures to feel embarrassed and respond angrily and unprofessionally to such images. For instance, if a company that has employees from different ethnicities chooses to use an image of a shouting Asian or Latin American to demonstrate how not to respond to instances of racism or sexism in the workplace, the Asian and/or Latin American employees at that company will definitely feel uncomfortable with that kind of image portraying them as unruly and loud, and that might affect those people's full participation in the evaluation process.

2. **Involving marginalized groups in the processes:** As it turns out, many organizations only include marginalized groups in the data collection process. Once their opinions and ideas have been gathered, the affected groups probably won't know what happens to them—whether their organizations are acting on the useful suggestions they have provided

or have decided, as usual, to ignore them. This is why it is important to involve the representatives of marginalized groups in data collection, data processing, reporting, decision-making, and consultation. Through this approach, they can feel confident that their concerns are being treated seriously by their organizations and they can hope for better and more inclusive working experiences.

3. **Minimizing bias in all its forms:** Organizations should make efforts to minimize any forms of bias in their DEI evaluations or assessments, beginning with using a respectful and appropriate tone in designing evaluation questions and illustrations. They also need to exercise caution while reporting the outcomes of the evaluation; they shouldn't paint one group as bad while elevating the ideals of the other. It is wrong to stigmatize one subgroup by using language it considers inappropriate or using images that depict annoying stereotypes.

7.2 Establishing a DEI Vision and Organizational Language

7.2.1 Establishing a DEI vision

An organization needs to establish a clear and understandable DEI vision that will be enshrined in its constitution, operational manuals, and workplace documents. Simply defined, an organization's DEI vision is a bold statement that summarizes or outlines how the organization plans to operate in a diverse and inclusive working environment where everyone feels welcomed and fully integrated into the system.

To better understand what a DEI vision really looks like, here are a couple of examples from two global organizations:

1. **Coca-Cola, Inc.'s DEI vision statement:** "Diversity, equity, and inclusion are at the heart of our values and our growth strategy and play an important part in our company's success. We leverage the remarkable diversity of people across the world to achieve our purpose of refreshing the world and making a difference. Our aspiration is not only to mirror the diversity of the communities where we operate but also to lead and advocate for a better shared future. We aspire to create a workforce that mirrors the markets we serve. It is our aspiration by 2030 to have women hold 50% of senior leadership roles at the company and in the U.S. to have race and ethnicity representation reflect national census data at all levels. We enable an inclusive culture where our employees thrive. These ambitions are part of how we create a better-shared future for people everywhere, empowering access to equal opportunities and building inclusion and belonging, both in our workplaces and in society. We create affinity, allyship, community, and celebration and use our brands to inspire and advocate for inclusion."

2. **Johnson & Johnson's DEI vision statement:** "Diversity at Johnson & Johnson is about each of our unique perspectives. It's about us, our colleagues, and the world we care for – all backgrounds, beliefs, abilities, and the entire range of human experience. We are building on our strong foundation to meet the needs of the evolving world and to make meaningful change at Johnson & Johnson and for society as a whole. Be yourself, and change the world. Our vision at Johnson & Johnson is for every person to use their unique experiences, abilities, and backgrounds, together – to spark solutions that create a better, healthier world.

Diversity, Equity & Inclusion at Johnson & Johnson means we all belong."

These two examples of DEI visions reveal how Coca-Cola and Johnson & Johnson are handling their DEI initiatives, creating an inclusive ecosystem where all their employees can feel valued, respected, fully engaged, and appropriately rewarded or compensated for all their meaningful contributions to the growth of these organizations.

7.2.2 Crafting and promoting organizational DEI language

It is not enough though for an organization to draft a powerful DEI vision statement, there must be genuine efforts toward initiating and implementing a structural change within the organization's hierarchies and operations. One of the best ways to accomplish this is to craft a new organizational language devoid of racial slurs, demeaning utterances, and disrespectful name-callings. The instances of workplace harassment and toxicity are still pretty much prevalent. According to some recent statistics published by the American Psychological Association (APA), the current situations in some American workplaces where DEI principles are fully embraced or implemented are quite alarming:

1. More than one-quarter (29%) of workers strongly (10%) or somewhat (19%) agreed that they do not matter to their employer.

2. Just over one-quarter (26%) said their employer does not respect their personal boundaries.

3. However, nearly one in five strongly (6%) or somewhat (13%) disagreed with the statement, "When I'm at work, I feel like I belong."

4. More females (23%) reported a toxic workplace than males (15%).

5. In 2023, 22% of workers experienced harassment at work in the past 12 months.

6. 92% of workers said it is very (57%) or somewhat (35%) important to them to work for an organization that values their emotional and psychological well-being.

Harassment, racism, sexism, and ageism become rife in a working environment where there is no unifying organizational DEI language, and this can tremendously affect employees' emotional and psychological well-being, including their mental health. So, what is an organizational DEI language? It is simply the nature of language adopted by an organization aimed at promoting and/or encouraging full-scale DEI implementation among its employees.

Some of the characteristics of well-scripted organizational DEI language is that:

- It should be respectful and edifying, not derogatory.

- It shouldn't be sexist, ageist, or racist.

- It should be gender-neutral.

- It should be historically and culturally conscious.

- It should be accessible to all employees (not technical jargon or terminologies that all employees cannot understand).

The American Psychological Association (APA) updates its Inclusive Language Guide every year, which offers some sensible suggestions about inclusive language that organizations can adopt and publicize to their employees.

| Table 7.1 | Some examples of APA inclusive language (2024) | |

Term to avoid	Suggested alternative	Comment
the poor/ poor people	people whose incomes are below the federal poverty threshold	As always, there should be room for nuance and flexibility when using these terms. Many people find the terms "low-class" and "poor" pejorative. Conversely, class solidarity exists in "poor people's movements" and many individuals proudly identify as "working class." Define specific income brackets and levels if possible (e.g., "low income").
low-class people/ lower class people	people who are of low SES/ socioeconomic status/	
blue-collar worker	skilled trades worker/ manual laborer	These terms are considered somewhat outdated as they originated in the early 20th century (Harris, 2022; Wilkie, 2019).
white-collar worker	salaried professional	
born a girl, born female/ born a boy, born male	assigned female at birth (AFAB)/ assigned male at birth (AMAB)	

Term to avoid	Suggested alternative	Comment
The word "Latino" is gendered (i.e., "Latino" is masculine, and "Latina" is feminine)	The term "Latine" is gender inclusive.	
wheelchair-bound/ person confined to a wheelchair/ cripple/ invalid/ gimp	wheelchair user/ a person who uses a wheelchair/ a person with a physical disability	Avoid language that uses pictorial metaphors, negativistic terms that imply restriction, and slurs that insult or disparage a particular group. As with other diverse groups, insiders in disability culture may use these terms with one another; it is not appropriate for an outsider (e.g., a nondisabled person) to use these terms.
make your voice heard	express your perspective/ opinion	
the elderly/ elderly people/ the aged/ aging dependents/ seniors/ senior citizens	older adults/ older people/ persons 60 years and older/ older population/ older individuals/	Avoid language that promotes stereotypes that "other" older adults. However, please note that in certain cultures, the term "Elder" is considered an honorific.

Source: APA Inclusive Language Guide

It may appear doable and quick to incorporate appropriate organizational language into an environment that has already put in place certain aspects of DEI policies. However, the case is entirely different from a workplace that has no existing DEI practices. To introduce organizational language or any structural change in an organization, Waters et al. (2023) proposed a four-stage model, which includes planning, committing to change, implementing change, and evaluating progress for the desired change.

Organizations must understand that a rude manager or supervisor will change overnight and suddenly become well-natured and respectful until there are guidelines set up to correct his/her abnormal behaviors. The same thing goes for racist coworkers who target people who are not from their race or ethnicity. Once DEI rules of engagement have been established in an organization, employees will be required to play by the newly introduced DEI principles or face being relieved of their job or position in the organization.

7.3 Formulating SMART Objectives

A significant aspect of an organization's DEI strategy is to formulate "SMART" objectives, whereby "SMART" is an acronym for specific, measurable, attainable, relevant, and time-based.

| Figure 7.1 | Formulated "SMART" objectives |

Source: Adapted from fossilconsulting.com

This entails that the organization needs to set specific goals or objectives that are measurable, attainable, relevant, and time-based.

Here are three examples of DEI SMART objectives that an organization may want to put together in order to facilitate its DEI initiatives:

1. **To increase the number of unrepresented employees in leadership**

   Every company has different communities or subgroups in its fold, as already explained in this chapter. When there is unequal representation for all the subgroups in a company, it may cause an imbalance in leadership. This can affect the quality of decisions made by those who don't belong to the marginalized subgroups, an issue that may threaten the successful implementation of DEI ideals in that company.

Applying the SMART goal technique, this is how the above-mentioned problem can be practically resolved:

- Specific: Form a diverse leadership that duly represents all subgroups.

- Measurable: Discover some existing roles or positions that someone from the unrepresented subgroups can fill or create an entirely new position or role for this purpose.

- Achievable: Investigate the diverse backgrounds and cultures within the company where the leadership candidates can be sourced from.

- Realistic: Deliberately increase the number of unrepresented subgroups in the leadership ranks.

- Time-bound: Undertake this goal within 3-6 months.

2. **To increase the number of partnerships with minority-owned businesses:**

   Organizations cannot afford to lose a segment of their customer base, and one of the proactive approaches for maintaining mutually beneficial interactions with culturally diverse clientele or customers is to increase the number of partnerships with minority-owned businesses.

Applying SMART principles, this issue can be professionally handled as follows:

- Specific: Systematically add more minority-owned businesses as partners.

- Measurable: Outline the criteria for selecting these partners based on their alignment with the organization long-term visions and mission.

- Achievable: Explore the possibility of finding partners that are suitable for this business engagement.

- Realistic: Begin the business engagement partners as trials and monitor the metrics and KPIs to see which of them can stay with the organization for a long time.

- Time-bound: Give this objective about 12 months to be accomplished.

3. **To recruit more culturally diverse talent and create a truly DEI-compliant workforce:**

Some organizations may want to change course and intentionally increase the number of culturally diverse hires or employees in their workforce. This exercise can also be undertaken with the application of the SMART goal, as described below:

- Specific: To bring in new hires that cut across different ages, cultures, races, genders, etc.

- Measurable: Achieve a 25% increase in diverse recruitment.

- Achievable: By presenting itself as an organization that welcomes all people irrespective of their demographics, the organization can draw culturally diverse job candidates to its job advertisements.

- Realistic: If the organization currently has a 5% diverse workforce, it needs to expand that by 20%. It will need to post jobs where culturally diverse job candidates can see them. More specifically, the job roles/positions should be framed in a way that culturally diverse job applicants can feel they are qualified enough to apply to them.

- Time-bound: This is slated to be done within the next 6-12 months.

There are other areas of an organization's operations that can be improved with the application of SMART goal-setting.

7.4 Establishing Accountability Metrics

A company can monitor the progress of its DEI practices and measure its success by utilizing a set of DEI metrics and key performance indicators (KPIs). Highlighted below are nine metrics and KPIs specifically utilized by DEI professionals to detect how their organizations are faring as far as DEI implementations are concerned:

1. **Diversity index:** This is usually referred to as the foundational KPI, and it aims to quantify the percentage of representation of diverse demographics within an organization. It reveals the exact number of employees belonging to the subgroups within an organization.

2. **Equity ratio:** This metric is used to identify the level of equity among employees of a company irrespective of their cultural backgrounds. It serves to see if everyone in that company is treated fairly and each of them has equal access to career advancement and the company's resources.

3. **Inclusion score**: This is an essential KPI in the sense that it reveals the extent of inclusivity within an organization's

workforce. It will reveal the level of employees' participation in their organization's processes, such as in decision-making and management duties.

4. **Turnover rate among underrepresented groups:** As its name implies, this metric hopes to identify the turnover rate among unrepresented employees. Do they stay long in that company or are leaving in droves due to uncomfortable working experiences?

5. **Pay equity:** This Pay Equity KPI attempts to detect any disparity in the employees' salaries. Are men paid more than their female counterparts? Are people from marginalized groups underpaid when compared with workers from other demographic groups within an organization?

6. **Promotion rates:** This metric is specifically used to discover if there is discrimination in the promotion rates. This will reveal if employees from the unrepresented groups are being shortchanged and denied their due promotions.

7. **Leadership representation:** This KPI aims to detect whether all subgroups within a company are duly represented at the company's management level.

8. **Supplier diversity:** This KPI helps organizations to know if there have been discriminatory practices in their supplier partnership programs. To maintain good customer retention and revenue, every organization aspires to have at least a partnership with a minority-owned business that serves each of their customer segment or demographics.

9. **Employee resource group (ERG) engagement:** This is an important KPI because it reveals the level of engagement of employees, mostly those from marginalized groups with

their organizations' resources like educational materials, career development programs, etc.

7.5 Learning How to Promote Openness and Clarity

In addition to having a great DEI strategy, it is the sole responsibility of organizations to still take some legitimate steps in promoting openness and clarity about their sundry DEI principles. Some of the approaches that can be adopted in the promotion of DEI policies include but are not limited to the following:

1. **Improved hiring practices:** It is advisable that organizations transform their hiring practices. They should change the manner they recruit and vet candidates. Moreover, when onboarding new employees, they should emphasize the importance of complying with in-house DEI policies. Some organizations go as far as threatening to fire any new hires that undermine the integrity and human rights of their colleagues.

2. **Company-wide education:** It is important to educate everyone in the company about the ideals of diversity, equity, and inclusion (DEI), from the low-ranked employees to the C-suite leaders.

3. **Creating an inclusive workplace:** The most effective way to spread the good message of DEI is to create an inclusive workplace for all employees. This entails that the organizations and their management must take every action to acknowledge and celebrate employee differences. Creating a workspace where everyone's voice is listened to

and valued will systematically improve interrelationships among employees from different cultural backgrounds.

4. **Anti-discrimination policies:** It is sensible for an organization to periodically review any existing anti-discrimination policies so as to update all its employees that discrimination against one another is a serious and punishable offense.

5. **Channels for grievances:** It is reasonable to segment employee surveys and other avenues for obtaining information about their experiences in the workplace. Giving employees the opportunity to complain about something they don't like about their workplace can help the organization they work for take quick steps to ameliorate whatever grievances they might have.

6. **Consistent communication:** Organizations should consistently communicate their DEI goals to their employees, whether through a weekly newsletter or intranet chatroom.

7. **Mentorship program:** By setting up a DEI mentorship program, an organization can recommend employees with limited knowledge of DEI ideals to attend such a mentorship program that will help them change their discriminatory tendencies.

Chapter 8

Dedication to Diversity

In this chapter, we take a cognizance look at the perennial issue of gender pay parity and its negative impacts on any organization's willingness to fully implement DEI initiatives. It is important that company-wide training on unconscious bias and cultural insensitivity be routinely conducted and performance evaluation measures established so as to create a diverse cross-generational workforce and support the use of preferred pronouns.

Key learning objectives should include the reader's understanding of the following:

- Gender pay parity
- When to conduct training on unconscious bias and cultural insensitivity
- Creating a diverse workforce across generations
- Inventing a mechanism for performance evaluation
- Supporting the utilization of preferred pronouns

8.1 Gender Pay Parity

For the past decades, notably between 1982 and 2022, organizations in the United States have taken significant steps to ensure that men and women are offered fair compensation for undertaking equal amounts of jobs at the same location. This is a commendable effort geared toward actualizing DEI objectives in corporate America, but more actions still need to be taken.

According to Pew Research Center (2023), American women are being paid 82 cents for every dollar men receive in 2022. This was comparable to 2002 when women were paid 80 cents for every dollar men had got. This is simple math: It indicates that for nearly two decades, American women's earnings increased by a tad, 2 cents. This development may be considered a good step in the right direction, bearing in mind that American women were shortchanged in 1982 when they were earning 65 cents to every dollar their male counterparts had received (Pew Research Center, 2023).

According to the World Economic Forum's Global Gender Pay Report 2023, almost all countries fall behind in closing the gender pay gap. This report, which investigated the issue of gender pay parity in 146 nations, indicates the countries still have a lot of work to do to ensure that men and women are paid fairly. It is assumed that it may take about 131 years to completely close the gender pay gap globally. As of now, North America (75% parity) trails behind Europe (at 76.3% parity), and the worst situation is seen in the Middle East and North Africa (at 62.6% parity) (World Economic Forum, 2023).

Santos and Klasen (2021) enumerated some of the problems associated with gender inequality for women, from facing economic woes to lacking the wherewithal to advance opportunities for their immediate families. Single mothers are mostly affected by this menace as they struggle to keep their family dynamics intact while stretching themselves to earn their livelihood. In old age, women are likely to experience extreme poverty and social exclusion as they have been unable to save enough for retirement.

Women in different workplaces across the United States are dissatisfied with being underpaid even though they are doing the same work as men. An organization, for instance, stands to lose immensely if its most dedicated and hardworking workforce—women—are demotivated for not being duly recognized for their tangible contributions at every level of the organization's operations.

In an article published in Harvard Business Review (HBR), Anderson, Bjarnadóttir, and Ross (2024) offered a comprehensive guideline that any company can adopt to close the gap for its female employees. First, they suggested that the organization should undertake a Pay Equity Analysis, which will reveal the discrepancies in employees' salaries, based on their genders. The Pay Equity Analysis model utilized by Anderson, Bjarnadóttir, and Ross (2024) compares each employee's actual salary with their expected (predicted) salary based on the pay equity model, and the difference was calculated.

Figure 8.1 reveals the distribution of income disparities as discovered by Anderson, Bjarnadóttir, and Ross (2024). They noticed that very few women were paid above their expected salaries and a large number of the women were underpaid when their actual pay was compared with their expected salary. No woman was among the top 10% best-paid, and only one woman was among the top 20% best-paid.

Figure 8.1   Difference in expected and actual salary

EMPLOYEES: ● WOMEN ● MEN

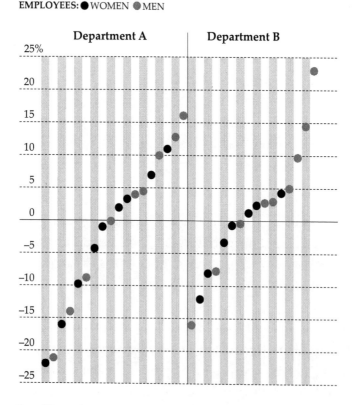

Source: David R. Anderson, Margret V. Bjarnadottir, and David Gaddis Ross, A better way for companies to address pay gaps. (2024, February 2). *Harvard Business Review.* https://hbr.org/2024/02/a-better-way-for-companies-to-address-pay-gaps

As shown in Figure 8.2, Anderson, Bjarnadóttir, and Ross (2024) demonstrated that focusing on addressing the pay gap for a select number of employees will not solve the pay disparity for any organization, even though it may lead to a slim reduction in the pay gap, but it will not completely close the gap.

| Figure 8.2 | Difference in expected and actual salary: focusing on select employees |

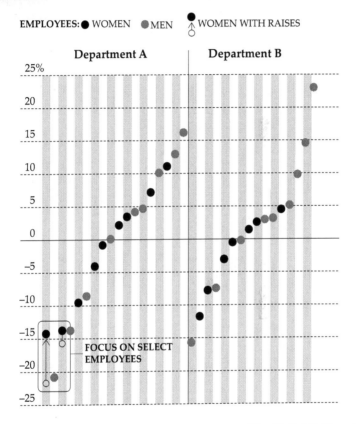

EMPLOYEES: ● WOMEN   ● MEN   ⊙ WOMEN WITH RAISES

Source: David R. Anderson, Margret V. Bjarnadottir, and David Gaddis Ross, A better way for companies to address pay gaps. (2024, February 2). *Harvard Business Review*. https://hbr.org/2024/02/a-better-way-for-companies-to-address-pay-gaps

Anderson, Bjarnadóttir, and Ross (2024) showed, in Figure 8.3 that the most sensible approach an organization can adopt in remediating the gap in salaries among its employees is to focus on "locus of pay inequity". This means that companies need to understand which parts of their salary structures are responsible for the acute disparities in salaries and then address the inequalities in those places or departments.

| Figure 8.3 | Difference in expected and actual salary: focusing on specific points of pay inequity |

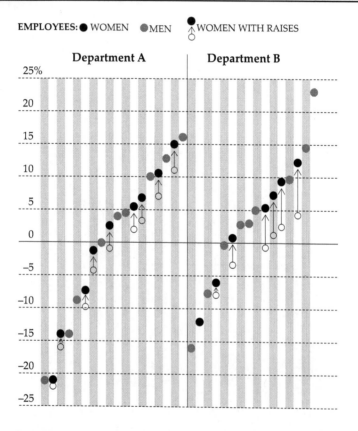

Source: David R. Anderson, Margret V. Bjarnadottir, and David Gaddis Ross, A better way for companies to address pay gaps. (2024, February 2). *Harvard Business Review*. https://hbr.org/2024/02/a-better-way-for-companies-to-address-pay-gaps

So, an organization should undertake the following procedures to systematically solve the pay gap among its employees:

1. **Identify the pay gap by department or experience level:** It is imperative to conduct an organization-wide pay gap analysis, done across all departments and experience or expertise levels. Through this approach, it is possible to discover how much disparity exists between the salaries of men and women working on the same projects within the departments.

2. **Discover where the different pay distributions are and fix the problem right there:** The initial pay gap analysis may reveal a clear picture of pay distributions among male and female employees with the same expertise level. Once discovered, it is advisable to fix the disparity in salaries right away by selecting the group of employees that are affected. This can be achieved by systematically reviewing the pay scale and fairly compensating those employees who have long been underpaid.

3. **Understand that data used to ameliorate this pay gap problem may have some limitations:** However, the data used to identify the pay gap may not be at all perfect. Therefore, company executives and managers are implored to utilize their discretion when handling this sensitive issue.

Sometimes the pay gap is influenced by biases prevalent in some departments within an organization. Efforts must first be concentrated on eliminating those unconscious biases so as to create a workplace that is fair, equal, and egalitarian.

8.2 When to Conduct Training on Unconscious Bias and Cultural Sensitivity

Deloitte (2021), a world-renowned consultant in organizational management, concurred that for an organization to fully realize the benefits of diversity, equity, and inclusion, it must conduct training to remove existing unconscious biases and cultural insensitivities from its fold. Unconscious biases, which are also called implicit biases, are automatic aversions or preferences people reflexively exhibit toward people from other genders, races, demographics, etc. For a white manager to believe that an Asian American isn't worth being paid $350,000 a year despite being qualified and experienced for the job is a typical example of an unconscious bias.

Sometimes some company executives or managers who are biased don't actually know they are; they may think they are just stating the obvious or repeating the long-held but unwritten prejudices held against people from certain races, genders, demographics, etc. One of those common stereotypic views harbored against female CEOs is that they are too emotional, soft, and weak to manage organizational challenges. When eventually they manage to become CEOs, female leaders are often shortchanged and underpaid comparable to their male counterparts.

Deloitte canvassed three strategic approaches for managing unconscious biases and cultural insensitivities:

1. **Setting up DEI training:** Organizations are expected to first undertake DEI assessment to identify any weaknesses

and skill gaps in their existing DEI practices. Once those imperfections have been discovered, they should immediately activate DEI training or learning strategies to address those issues in order to ensure that their DEI aspirations are in line with their organizational visions/ mission and business goals. At this stage, it may be advisable to create an entirely new and effective DEI curriculum (if none was available before), choose the most convenient delivery methods (whether by in-class lectures, virtual or e-class learning, or focus group deliberations), and incorporate an assessment to gauge learners' understanding of the subject matter. Some companies have in-house educational programs delivered weekly or monthly to employees' emails, intranet accounts, and mobile devices to consistently reinforce DEI principles.

2. **Promoting personal and organization-wide DEI compliance:** Organizations should foster a DEI-enabling atmosphere or ecosystem that facilitates personal DEI compliance. The rule of thumb is that if employees within an organization are personally motivated to practice and advance DEI ideals, respecting their colleagues irrespective of their race, demographic, or gender, it will be expressly easy for that organization to achieve its DEI ambitions. There is a common saying that a toxic working environment begins with just one toxic colleague, supervisor, manager, or executive who is narcissistic in nature and encourages others to act like him/her or give others free rein to undermine their colleagues' rights and freedom.

3. **Encouraging DEI fluency:** Far from being a sprint, consistent DEI practices indeed cover an organization's life cycle. To encourage DEI fluency, an organization needs

to create an environment where targeted DEI principles are consistently related to its employees. If the goal of implementing DEI initiatives is to reduce or eliminate the gender pay gap or expunge racial profiling among its employees, the organization must constantly remind its employees of the importance of not disrespecting their colleagues or managers and not underpaying women.

Every change in an organization brings about some positive transformations, and conducting DEI training to address the issues of unconscious bias and cultural insensitivity can cause an organization to:

1. **Create a diverse and inclusive workplace:** When DEI principles spread in a workplace, everyone in that environment will be considered a vital part of the system, irrespective of their gender, culture, or demographic. This can lead to great organizational performance and higher productivity.

2. **Embrace fairness in all its decision-making:** The primary reason companies are adopting DEI principles is to be able to make decisions devoid of partiality and inconsideration. Most astute company managers understand that employees perform at their best when they feel valued, equitably compensated, and motivated.

8.3 Creating a Diverse Workforce Across Generations

When her company was ranked the No.1 company on Refinitiv's Diversity & Inclusion Index, which identifies the 100 publicly traded companies with the most diverse and inclusive workplaces, Julie Sweet, the female CEO of Accenture reportedly said, "We are honored that Refinitiv has recognized Accenture's unwavering commitment to diversity and inclusion — it is essential to the growth of our business, our continued innovation and our ability to create 360° Value for our clients, our communities and all our stakeholders."

Creating a diverse, multigenerational workforce doesn't happen just overnight; it is a result of consistent effort at recognizing people's identities, respecting their values, and creating an environment for peaceful engagement, interactions, and co-existence. Julie Sweet, in her own words, has possibly disclosed how Accenture, established in 1989 (nearly 35 years ago) has been able to maintain a multigenerational, diverse workforce. She mentioned:

1. Diverse communities: Any organization that embodies or encourages a "We, Our, and Us" culture tends to have hyper-performing employees, because everyone in the organization sees each other as partner-in-progress working on a common organization. In this situation, there is no rancor or office politics that usually threatens cohesion and camaraderie among people working together.

2. Continued innovation: The 21st-century workplace faces countless challenges, some of which require innovative

approaches to overcome. Companies must be creative in their recruitment, training, and onboarding procedures in a way that people from different races, genders, demographics, etc. are evenly represented. Moreover, cutting-edge communications should be employed in constantly reminding all employees about their obligation to uphold DEI ideals.

3. Stakeholders' level-playing: When all stakeholders are appreciated, they will nurture a feeling of belongingness which, in turn, will motivate them to contribute greatly to the success of their organization. Stakeholders in a company come across different ages, genders, and demographics, and possess diverse skill sets and levels of expertise. By recognizing their efforts and equitably or fairly compensating them, an organization can, in the long term, maintain a diverse and multigenerational workforce that will uphold its values and visions.

8.4 Inventing a Mechanism for Performance Evaluation

How do organizations know if their DEI implementation is working? It is through performance evaluation. DEI performance evaluation can be defined as the process of assessing or measuring the performance of individuals, teams, and subgroups within an organization against laid-down expectations and outcomes in line with the organization's DEI initiatives.

To successfully undertake a DEI performance evaluation, it is important for the organization to collect, analyze, and interpret data to detect if its employees have been standing up for its DEI policies. Some of the merits of carrying out DEI performance evaluation are to improve any weak areas in the actualization of diversity, equity, and inclusion programs, promote accountability, and streamline decision-making. It is necessary for organizations to come up with a functional performance evaluation mechanism. While it is true that each company will invent its own performance evaluation process that aligns with its culture and DEI objectives, the most common performance assessment methodology involves:

- **Self-evaluation:** Employees will be given questionnaires, surveys, and other assessment tools to evaluate their own compliance with their organizations' DEI recommendations. Are they showing due respect to their colleagues? Are they working on reducing the extent of their unconscious biases?

- **360-degree evaluation:** This kind of evaluation requires collecting feedback from different sources within an organization, including subordinates, peers, managers, supervisors, and customers. This step is essential in order to draw up company-wide feedback that will be fed back into the system.

- **Program evaluation:** What makes a DEI program successful lies in the complete implementation of all the policies geared toward raising awareness about diversity and inclusion among employees, encouraging full participation in the drive, and creating an environment that facilitates cohesiveness at a workplace.

138   *Diversity, Equity, and Inclusion Essentials You Always Wanted To Know*

- **Team evaluation:** It is important to investigate if every member of the teams in an organization supports and advocates DEI goals. The main reason why companies struggle with their DEI initiatives is that if one team member happens to become unsupportive of the initiatives, his/her other colleagues might imitate him/her and frustrate all the efforts deployed toward establishing fairness and equality in such an environment. The worst-case scenario is if the opponent of the DEI program is a senior staff or an executive within the company.

- **Project evaluation:** While working on projects, people are expected to consistently observe DEI principles. This entails that no employee should be excluded from working on projects within the company or prevented from using their skills to execute projects based on their company's requirements. Assessing each project and the level of involvement of each employee on the team will reveal if some of them have been unduly barred from doing their job.

8.5 Supporting the Utilization of Preferred Pronouns

Nowadays, the workforce has become truly diverse and organizations need to embrace and support the utilization of pronouns at workplaces in order to provide a safe and inclusive environment.

www.vibrantpublishers.com

Table 8.1 reveals some of the gendered and gender-neutral pronouns utilized at various organizations.

Table 8.1	Gender-neutral pronouns

Getting to Know Gender-Neutral Pronouns!					
Traditional Masculine	He laughed	I called him	His eyes gleam	That is his	He likes himself
Traditional Feminine	She laughed	I called her	Her eyes gleam	That is hers	She likes herself
Gender Neutral (Singular They)	They laughed	I called them	Their eyes gleam	That is theirs	They like themself
Gender Neutral (Ze)	Ze laughed (pronounced: "zee" as in the letter 'z')	I called hir (pronounced: "here")	Hir eyes gleam (pronounced: "here")	That is hirs (pronounced: "here's")	Ze likes hirself (pronounced: "here-self")

Source: Adapted from https://buffer.com

The use of nonbinary pronouns "They" and "Ze" is done to address people with different gender entities, such as genderqueer and gender-fluid people. People with genderqueer identity don't exclusively identify as male or female; they could exhibit a gender identity in between or both. Similarly, people who are regarded to be gender fluid don't necessarily identify as a gender, and their gender may change over time.

For the 21st-century workplace to be considered inclusive, those who are assigned a gender identity or with no gender identity deserve to be respected and valued in spite of their gender orientation. There are three strategic approaches an organization can take to encourage the utilization of the appropriate pronouns among its employees:

- Ask every employer to identify their gender orientation beside their names. In this way, their colleagues will know how to properly address them using the right, inclusive pronouns.

- For those who are gender fluid, when they are attending a meeting or workshop, it is important to ask everyone in attendance to introduce themselves and clearly state their gender identities to avoid misuse of pronouns.

- To encourage the utilization of the appropriate pronouns, all employees in an organization must be subjected to ongoing training where they will learn how to address and interact with people based on their unique gender types.

Chapter 9

Dedication to Fairness

This chapter focuses on what organizations need to do in order to promote fairness in all ramifications of their operations. This involves revising their recruitment policy practices and blending their onboarding procedures so that every employee nurtures a sense of belonging. It is equally important to set up an in-house DEI task force to foster inclusive leadership and consistently communicate equity objectives and milestones to all stakeholders.

Key learning objectives should include the reader's understanding of the following:

- Revising recruitment policy practices
- Blending an onboarding experience
- Launching a DEI task force
- Fostering inclusive leadership
- Communicating equity objectives and milestones

9.1 Revising Recruitment Policy Practices

Organizations need to take decisive action to reform their hiring procedures so as to foster a holistically diverse and inclusive workplace. In circumstances where DEI practices are found lacking, it's critical to revise recruitment policies in a way that will reflect diversity, equity, and inclusion (DEI) for all stakeholders.

Why is it imperative for an organization to revise its recruitment policy practices?

- Eliminating bias: It is necessary to review and update the existing recruitment processes by identifying and eliminating any unconscious biases.

- **Enhancing innovation**: A company that has a large number of employees or teams can creatively innovate its operational systems by allowing diverse opinions from different people working on a particular task or project.

- **Boosting reputation**: Companies with great DEI reputations can easily attract top talent from different backgrounds, a move that will boost their competitiveness and recognition.

- **Legal and ethical compliance**: Organizations in the United States are expected to continuously update their hiring processes to ensure strict compliance with or adherence to all anti-discrimination statutes and laws.

- **Customer-based reflection**: By paying attention to its customers' needs and preferences, an organization can retain or expand its customer base, because consumers feel satisfied when they are served by people who look like them.

9.1.1 Strategies for revising recruitment policies

Shore et al. (2018) believed that conscious or concerted efforts are required at the organizational level to modify the existing hiring practices so as to guarantee a full implementation of DEI ideals. Therefore, to effectively revise recruitment policies, companies should take the following strategies into consideration:

- **Blind recruitment processes**

  To avoid unconscious bias from influencing recruitment outcomes, it is advisable to remove applicants' personal information from resumes during the initial screening process, such as names, gender, age, and photos. For instance, Deloitte used a blind hiring procedure early on, which increased the diversity of the candidates it was considering.

- **Diverse sources**

  Organizations should utilize job boards that specifically target underrepresented groups, attend diversity-focused job fairs, and collaborate with a variety of professional associations. For example, Intel demonstrated the significance of having a culturally diverse talent base when it set up "Intel Diversity in Technology Initiatives" in partnerships with historically black colleges and universities (HBCUs) and Hispanic-serving Institutions (HSIs).

- **Bias training for recruiters**

  It is advisable for companies to periodically organize training for hiring managers and HR staff in order to discover and reduce any biases they may be unconsciously having against others.

- **Inclusive job descriptions**

  Buffer, a company that helps small businesses manage their social media accounts, revamped its hiring procedures by removing from its job descriptions any words, phrases, or expressions that are unnecessary and gender-based to attract a pool of culturally diverse job applicants. In principle, companies should avoid utilizing jargon, expressions, or phrases that are racially discriminating and gender-specific in their job descriptions and postings. The essence of DEI is to create a working environment that is welcoming to all races, genders, etc. Internal metrics and responsibility

  One sensible approach for a company to keep an eye on how it is faring in its DEI practices is to regularly evaluate its internal DEI metrics throughout its hiring processes. By taking this step, it will be possible for such a company to identify areas where it has failed to meet its specific DEI goals. Moreover, leaders within an organization should be held responsible for upholding their company's DEI policies. Salesforce, for example, has consistently disclosed its yearly DEI progress in its annual reports, causing even its C-suite executives to be well aware of its respect for diversity.

9.1.2 Case studies: Organizations modernizing hiring procedures

1. **Microsoft:**
   Microsoft is one of the leading beacons of diversity in the workforce. As part of its DEI strategies, the company put in place diverse interview panels, promoted DEI initiatives, and reached out to various communities for culturally diverse job candidates. This explains why a large percentage of the company's employees today are women and minorities. In 2014, Microsoft appointed Satya Nadella, an Indian-American, to become its Chairman/CEO.

2. **IBM:**
   IBM made its recruiting managers undergo comprehensive bias training and incorporated AI into its hiring procedures. These two approaches have helped the company achieve diversity in its talent pool. IBM's AI systems, in particular, are programmed to identify biases in the company's recruitment exercise so that they can be addressed with immediate effect.

3. **Accenture:**
   Accenture projected that by 2025 its workforce would have been truly diverse. Some of the strategic steps the company took to become truly diverse include using inclusive job descriptions, utilizing employee sourcing services that welcome people from different cultures, genders, etc., and conducting bias training for its managers. Over the years, Accenture has recorded a significant achievement in the areas of its gender and racial diversity.

9.1.3 Steps for implementing revised recruitment policies

1. **Perform an audit:**
   It may be necessary for organizations to perform a periodic audit of their hiring processes so as to discover any biased practices. In this case, it will be possible to discover if their existing hiring systems are tainted with biases. This may require obtaining vital information from interviewers, interviewees, job candidates/applicants, and hires.

2. **Establish clear objectives:**
   Recruiters should be encouraged to set clear, attainable DEI goals during their hiring processes. By doing this, they will be able to monitor their progress, meet deadlines, and perform within their previously established accountability frameworks.

3. **Develop and implement new practices:**
   It may be advisable for organizations to adopt and implement refined hiring practices. This may involve introducing various sourcing methods as well as incorporating blind hiring practices. Using uniform interview procedures can reduce any act of intentional biases. If an organization's current job descriptions are restrictive, they can be updated to be inclusive enough for all applicants to feel encouraged to apply to jobs they are qualified for.

4. **Provide training:**
   It is imperative for organizations to provide regular and impactful training for all members of their recruitment teams so that they can be fully aware of unconscious biases and sensibly avoid them. Sometimes it is necessary to

remind recruiters that they should operate within the ambits of their respective organizations' inclusive policies.

5. **Monitor and adjust:**
   By asking members of the recruitment team and job candidates for their opinions and reviewing the diversity metrics, it is possible for an organization to use the feedback and data obtained to systematically make adjustments or improvements in certain aspects of its recruitment process that might have been failing.

6. **Communicate commitment:**
   Organizations should endeavor to make their diversity commitments known to all stakeholders that are connected to their operations. This can be done through both internal and external channels of communication, emphasizing the progress made so far on DEI objectives, which has been instrumental in drawing a pool of diverse candidates to the organizations.

9.2 Blending an Onboarding Experience

Malik (2023) argued that creating an inclusive working environment requires revamping the current policies that have failed to achieve true diversity and inclusion within that environment. Establishing a culture of diversity, equity, and inclusion (DEI) in an organization requires a well-thought-out onboarding procedure. New hires need to be properly informed about the culture of value and mutual respect in place at the organization they are becoming part of. The primary goal of the DEI-focused onboarding procedure is to create an environment where all employees thrive, feel like they belong, and are fairly treated. These steps are required to guarantee that everyone equally succeeds in their assigned duties within the organization.

9.2.1 Significance of onboarding in DEI

Onboarding procedures at each organization are vital for introducing new employees into their organizations' DEI programs. Owing to its operational significance, it must be properly planned and executed with utmost care. The following are some of the strategic steps that should be taken into consideration:

- **The importance of setting the foundation:** Every new hire's first introduction into their organizational culture usually takes place during their onboarding process. It is the period they will learn, in detail, about how their new employer prioritizes DEI. This foundational knowledge is essential because the new hires will be instructed on how to comport themselves within the organization, by strictly following the organization's DEI policies and practices. As the saying goes, out of sight is out of mind; people won't naturally internalize or constantly remind themselves of organizational rules (in this case, DEI rules) that no one had ever taught them. Therefore, it is the responsibility of the onboarding team to ensure that the new hires fully comprehend their organization's DEI requirements while welcoming them with an open and inclusive working environment.

- **Encouraging workplace participation in DEI activities:** Establishing a workplace that is purely guided by DEI principles goes beyond onboarding. It is equally important that there should be on-the-job support for both the long-term employees and new hires to actively participate in promoting DEI requirements and activities at their organization. This approach is capable of helping organizations lower their attrition rates while retaining good, diverse talent. In other words, everyone should be welcome to participate in encouraging fairness and mutual respect at all times.

- **Enhancing output**: It is generally believed that a well-articulated onboarding program will empower new hires with the right information, resources, and skills they need to excel at their workplaces. However, what motivates new hires to actively contribute to DEI initiatives at their places of work is being valued. When they feel that their opinions count, they will be willing to come up with practical ideas to advance their organization's DEI expectations. In the course of this, many creative and innovative ideas may be born, which can be useful in improving their organization's overall business operations.

9.2.2 Key elements of a DEI-focused onboarding experience

Highlighted below are some key elements of a DEI-focused onboarding experience aimed at strengthening any organization's DEI policies, if properly implemented.

- **Comprehensive orientation programs:**
  Orientation programs for new hires should be comprehensive and comprise detailed information about the organization's DEI requirements, policies, and responsibilities. Having a deep understanding of how

DEI initiatives are implemented at their new companies can help new hires play by the rules. Teaching sensitive topics like cultural competency, inclusive communication, and unconscious bias may require using interactive and engaging training modules, where the new hires will be asked to physically participate in demonstrations to see how things should be done as they join the new organization.

- **Buddy systems and mentoring**

  Providing new hires with workplace buddies or mentors can go a long way to giving them a sense of belonging to the community. These mentors or friends can help new hires navigate the new working environment safely by offering encouragement, guidance, and suggestions about how to interact respectfully with their coworkers. In large organizations, new hires usually struggle with acclimatizing themselves to the demands of daily routine assignments and corporate culture responsibilities. It is, however, important that these buddies and mentors be drawn from diverse cultural backgrounds for the buddy system to become effective.

- **Ongoing feedback mechanisms**

  Organizations should understand that recently hired staff should not be left unattended. For example, it is necessary to check on them every now and then to detect how they are coping or responding to DEI guidelines in their respective departments within the organization. They should be given anonymous surveys and questionnaires, digital or paper (whichever works best for them). They may be able to provide useful insights into their post-onboarding experiences which can be used in improving the entire recruitment process at that organization.

- **Cultural competence training**

  One of the main objectives of the DEI department is to regularly organize cultural competence training for new hires and the existing staff that will emphasize inclusive attitudes and diversity awareness. It is advisable that this kind of training is customized to suit each organization's DEI requirements. It may also be reasonable to utilize unique learning materials that address the organization's DEI needs in relation to its demographics.

- **Accessibility to resources**

  When preparing onboarding materials, it is simply practical to make them available in multiple formats accessible by different categories of users. They should be in large print, braille, and digital formats, based on employees' preferences. In this way, employees with disabilities will not feel unattended. All other instructional materials must be accessible, too, and support individual and group usage. There should be internal DEI networks comprising employees based on their ranks, departmental affiliations, and demographics.

9.2.3 Benefits of DEI-focused onboarding

In a study conducted for Glassdoor by Brandon Hall Group and released in 2015 as a report titled, "The True Cost of a Bad Hire," it was revealed that well-articulated onboarding procedures increase productivity by 70% and the retention of new hires by 82% (Laurano, 2015). These statistical figures show the apparent benefits of DEI initiatives as explained below:

- **Improving the image of the company**

  Organizations that embrace DEI principles and undertake inclusive onboarding procedures are likely going to get positive press and rank high on DEI rankings. Highly qualified job candidates from unrepresented groups often seek to work for such companies. In the long run, DEI-focused organizations can greatly improve their image and have the blessing of attracting intelligent and innovative employees.

- **Increasing originality and creativity**

  It is a fact that an inclusive workplace promotes cooperation among all employees. When this happens, employees can freely exchange original and creative ideas with one another in a way that will benefit their organization. Employees who feel respected and recognized for their wonderful contributions to the growth of their organization will be willing to offer more diverse viewpoints and useful insights into how their organization can progress and achieve its organizational objectives.

- **Boosting retention and loyalty of employees**

  Employees are usually obliged to be loyal to organizations that make them feel welcome. Moreover, they will continue working for such a company long-term rather than looking elsewhere to get recognized and respected. As a matter of fact, inclusive practices and well-executed onboarding procedures can help organizations save on recruiting and training new staff.

9.3 Launching a DEI Task Force

A diversity, equity, and inclusion (DEI) task force is a strategic initiative established by organizations to promote and maintain their DEI policies. The primary function of the DEI task force, which comprises a group of employees within the organization, is to ensure that the organization's DEI principles are incorporated into every facet of its operations. This section takes a cognizance look at the possible merits, responsibilities, and procedures for establishing a functional DEI task force.

9.3.1 Benefits of a task force on DEI

- **It increases accountability and focus**: A DEI task force ensures that all departments within an organization focus on the same DEI ideals, promoting equity, inclusion, and diversity among employees and teams in those departments. This will eradicate a situation whereby DEI practices vary from one department to another. At the same time, the DEI task force will delegate certain DEI responsibilities to people in different departments as a way of holding them accountable for fulfilling organizational DEI requirements.

- **It fosters strategic implementation of DEI guidelines**: A DEI task force will push for a coordinated implementation of DEI guidelines in which all employees are expected to play active (assigned or unassigned) roles in encouraging fairness and inclusion at their organization. The task force will equally manage the budget or resources deployed for DEI causes, ensuring that those resources are allocated effectively to teams and/or individuals executing DEI-focused programs.

- **It increases representation**: When companies establish DEI task forces, their intentions are to genuinely create an inclusive working environment where all demographics are duly represented. In other words, the task force members are required to formulate policies and principles that acknowledge the needs and aspirations of all employees. They will also be required to welcome diverse views and perspectives from all employees while drawing up their organization's DEI policies. When everyone's viewpoints are properly considered, it will invoke a sense of belonging among underrepresented employees.

- **It enhances interaction**: When employees feel that their voices are heard, and their opinions are taken into consideration on vital issues concerning their working experience at the organization, they will be excited to participate in all DEI initiatives and share regular information about their experiences and hopes. This high level of transparency in interactions is able to help the organization advance its DEI programs quickly. When employees interact with one another openly and frankly, it will build a strong bond among them and also help them to collaborate seamlessly on projects, tasks, and reporting.

- **It improves performance and innovation**: Organizations that adopt DEI principles are generally believed to do better than their competitors in the same industry. One of the reasons for this admirable achievement is that any

organization that truly practices diversity, equity, and
inclusion is able to have access to and utilize diverse
talent that contributes meaningfully and innovatively to
the development of their organization. Such a company
will also attain high employee satisfaction; and by
extension, happy employees will do everything in their
power to make their company's customers happy,
too, thereby increasing customer loyalty towards their
organization.

9.3.2 Additional responsibilities of the DEI task force

In addition to the statutory duties of the DEI task force described
above, there are other responsibilities they are expected to carry
out at their respective organizations. Some of them are outlined
below:

1. **To evaluate the current situation**: To determine the current
   situation of DEI programs and initiatives at a company,
   the task force members may need to compile relevant
   information by surveying employees to identify a number
   of issues they are grappling with, such as discovering any
   instances of pay parity, lack of satisfaction in their jobs,
   delayed promotions, etc. This auditing process is necessary
   for unearthing critical DEI issues within an organization. It
   is basically conducted to discover apparent strengths and
   weaknesses in an organization's DEI policies, culture, and
   DEI implementation.

2. **To establish objectives and goals**: On most occasions, it is
   the duty of the DEI task force to design DEI initiatives or
   policies, describe the expected goals/objectives, and outline
   the metrics for measuring the progress. This may require

creating a plan that will highlight the exact procedures for achieving the DEI goals, the pertinent materials to be used in the process, and the deadlines for each procedure/step.

3. **To develop and implement initiatives**: In addition to drafting the organizational DEI policies, the task force is also expected to champion its smooth implementation. Some organizations empower their DEI task forces to periodically run programs or initiatives aimed at promoting diversity, equity, and inclusion, such as Employee Resource Groups (ERGs), mentorship programs, DEI training, etc.

4. **To observe and carry out the necessary documentation**: By monitoring how employees are holding up their organization's DEI principles, the task force can document their actions in order to identify strengths and weaknesses in complying with organization-wide DEI practices. This information may be documented and communicated to the senior management staff who are keenly interested in knowing the true picture of DEI implementation at the organization. By updating them with weekly, monthly, or quarterly DEI reports, the C-suite executives will be able to incorporate the results into their overall decision-making.

5. **To increase knowledge and informed consciousness**: Through well-structured courses and training, the DEI task force can internally promote awareness about diversity, equity, and inclusion among employees. It is helpful that employees have some knowledge of important subjects such as cultural competency, unconscious bias, and inclusive leadership.

6. **To involve the stakeholders**: It requires concerted efforts to successfully implement DEI programs at any organization. This means that all the stakeholders should be proactively

involved in every step of the DEI campaign. Sometimes it may be expedient for the DEI task forces to hold sessions with both internal and external stakeholders like employees, management team, customers, clients, community members, etc. This kind of collaboration can produce great ideas that can be utilized in DEI implementation within the concerned organization.

9.3.3 Steps to Launch a DEI task force

For organizations that aspire to launch their own DEI task force, here are some essential steps that must be followed:

1. **Get leadership support and commitment**
   A task force cannot operate on its own without the full backing of the management team. Therefore, the first step in establishing one is to receive initial support and commitment from the senior leadership. Obtaining this mandate will empower the task force to operate within the organization's vision for fairness and inclusion among its workforce. It must be stated that the DEI task force isn't a new department under HR; it is simply a group of carefully selected individuals (employees) whose task is to ensure that their organization's DEI principles are observed and implemented. So, at every step of their operations, a DEI task force needs a strong commitment from their organization's leadership.

2. **Outline the goals and scope**
   This involves describing in detail what the task force will be doing. It is also important to highlight their authority and limitations. Therefore, a DEI task force is not expected to come up with entirely new ideas other than those already

enshrined in their organization's existing DEI policies. Although task force members may offer suggestions about how to improve some defects in their organization's current DEI practices, such new ideas are subject to approval by the senior leadership.

3. **Choose the members of the task force**

    To guarantee a wide range of viewpoints, assemble a diverse group of members from different departments, levels, and backgrounds. Select people who have a strong interest in DEI, are knowledgeable about DEI, and are dedicated to bringing about change inside the company.

4. **Formulate a charter**

    Draft a charter outlining the task force's objectives, roles, and responsibilities as well as its operational guidelines. To formally establish the task force's mandate, get senior leadership to approve the charter.

5. **Perform a DEI audit**

    It is crucial to conduct a DEI audit on the existing policies and practices in place at an organization. It is possible, through this audit, to identify any weaknesses in the implementation of the organization's current DEI activities. It is important to obtain both quantitative and qualitative data via surveys, focus groups, and interviews. The audit should reveal insightful information about employees' experiences and practices as indicated in their organization's DEI policies.

6. **Formulate a strategy**

    What is the primary strategy to be adopted by the DEI task force in executing their duties? It is helpful to have a strategy that will clearly describe the necessary steps to be taken, set the deadlines for each activity, and recommend the appropriate materials to be used for each training exercise. The strategy must consider the organization's DEI needs as well as focus on certain areas that require urgent improvements.

7. **Put initiatives into practice**
   The DEI efforts should be strictly carried out in accordance with the formulated strategy. All the employees should be actively engaged in the process so that they can have a sense of belonging to the organization. To actualize all DEI programs, it may be necessary to secure adequate funds for all the activities to be undertaken.

8. **Observe and assess**
   It is imperative for the DEI task force to establish metrics for assessing how their efforts are progressing. By observing the positive outcomes of DEI initiatives in employees' actions, the task force can appreciate that their efforts are yielding remarkable results. Moreover, they will also be able to identify areas where they need to make some adjustments to their strategies.

9. **Transparency and reporting**
   As previously discussed in this section, the senior leadership of most organizations expected to be briefed from time to time about the advancement of DEI practices in their organizations. As such, they should be updated on a regular basis, and the reporting must be transparent and reliable. To continue enjoying unwavering support and commitment from the management team, the DEI task force is expected to be open and direct about their achievements, challenges, and plans when communicating with the senior management.

9.4 Fostering Inclusive Leadership

It takes inclusive leadership to genuinely promote diversity, equity, and inclusion in any organization. In addition to fully supporting DEI policies, DEI-focused leadership entails creating a fair working environment where everyone feels welcomed, can freely contribute their quotas, and have their voices heard. This requires establishing appropriate DEI guidelines that can encourage employees to regard one another with mutual respect and kindness.

9.4.1 What is inclusive leadership?

Inclusive leadership is a distinctive characteristic of leaders who sincerely value diversity and inclusion whereby all employees in their organizations are given equal opportunities and recognition. Inclusive leaders are known for opposing any culture of partiality, oppression, and prejudice. Instead, they consistently champion equality, welcome diverse viewpoints and contributions, and wholly support the full implementation of DEI policies within their folds.

Every organization that aspires to grow and be recognized publicly for giving every employee an equal chance to thrive and succeed must have an inclusive leader. Other attributes of inclusive leaders include but are not limited to the following:

- **Self-awareness**

  Inclusive leaders are a group of self-aware individuals. They understand their own weaknesses when it comes to DEI ideals but they constantly seek ways to improve in areas they are found wanting. As a matter of fact, they seek consultations on how to overcome their own unconscious biases and prejudices.

- **Empathy**

  Leaders considered to be inclusive often take good care of their team members' well-being and growth. They are attentive to their complaints, provide much-needed solutions to their problems, and offer necessary assistance whenever required by their team members.

- **Cultural competency**

  Apart from embracing employees from diverse demographics, cultures, and identities, inclusive leaders sensibly conduct themselves in a manner that shows due respect to everyone, irrespective of their cultural backgrounds.

- **Fearlessness**

  For the fact that not all members of the senior management team really care about DEI practices, so, it becomes an act of courage and risk-taking for any of them to boldly stand up in support of full DEI implementation at their organization. Therefore, an inclusive leader must demonstrate a great deal of fearlessness to be able to fight injustices, recognize the uniqueness and contributions of underrepresented groups, and actively promote practices that will improve their well-being.

- **Dedicated to equity**

  Everyone who has ever worked for inclusive leaders understands that they are good at removing barriers that could have frustrated employees from underrepresented demographics. By doing so, every employee at their organization will have equal access to opportunities and resources based on their rank and experience.

- **Collaboration**

  Inclusive leaders take it upon themselves to encourage camaraderie among their employees or subordinates. They want them to collaborate smoothly on projects and cooperate with one another on DEI implementation so as to help their organization grow.

9.4.2 Benefits of inclusive leadership

Inclusive leadership usually brings about significant transformations in an organization. Highlighted below are some of the impacts of inclusive leadership on an organization's operations:

- **Improved team performance**

  According to Shore et al. (2018), inclusive leadership can lead to unprecedented team performance. By establishing a cohesive working environment where individual contributions and team engagement are routinely encouraged, employees will do everything in their power to advance their organization's corporate objectives while achieving their own or teams' professional goals.

- **Motivated innovation**

  Malik (2023) posited that inclusive leaders are capable of motivating every team member, irrespective of their cultural background or gender to offer innovative and creative ideas that will grow their organizations. When valued and respected, employees tend to put most of their energy into exchanging inventive solutions with one another and advancing their organizations' ambitions.

- **Boosted image of the organization**

    The public, customers, and partners always consider favorably any organization that has an inclusive culture— it indicates that the organization is managed by a group of inclusive leaders, and this well-recognized reputation may attract businesses from potential partners to the organization as well as lead to genuine customer loyalty.

9.4.3 Techniques for promoting inclusive leadership

It is possible to promote inclusive leadership by adopting the following techniques:

- **Training and development**

    Leaders should be included in the ongoing DEI training and their courses should be customized so as to provide the much-needed informative knowledge about DEI research's recent findings and the best practices in their industry. Leaders can regularly be educated through webinars, seminars, workshops, books, etc. on themes such as conscious bias, DEI principles, and cultural competency.

- **Performance metrics and accountability**

    There should also be performance metrics on which leaders' DEI performances could be measured. To have a glimpse into their levels of commitment to DEI practices, leaders can be gauged on their employee engagement ratings, rates of retention of underrepresented groups in their organizations, and their active participation in DEI activities. There should be integrated key performance indicators (KPIs) by which leaders can always measure the effectiveness of their DEI policies.

- **Promote open communication**

  Establish safe spaces for open communication where staff members can express their opinions and experiences without worrying about facing consequences. It is likewise important to set up a feedback system such as using surveys or focus groups to obtain employees' feedback on the extent of inclusion in their respective departments.

9.5 Communicating Equity Objectives and Milestones

It is an attribute of a DEI-focused organization to prioritize communicating equity objectives and milestones to its employees. All stakeholders, including staff members, executives, clients, and the public must be informed, involved, and in agreement with the organization's DEI objectives for effective communication to occur. The following points entail the importance of communicating equity objectives and milestones:

- **Transparency and trust**

  Open and reliable communication can lead to trust or result in an unbreakable bond among employees. On most occasions, employees appreciate truths and transparent revelations about the true picture of DEI implementation at their organizations. It is easy for some mischievous members of senior management to mislead the public about the extent of DEI adoption in their organizations. However, this misinformation and lack of accountability will rather discourage employees of such organizations from putting in their best, when their senior management has failed to appreciate them and value their previous input.

- **Participation and engagement**

  A good approach for increasing employees' participation in DEI-related activities is to educate them about their organization's DEI expectations or requirements. By constantly encouraging them to be involved in DEI initiatives, employees will be able to increase their engagement with one another and with their leadership in order to advance their organization's DEI goals.

- **Motivation and morale**

  Staff members' morale can be boosted by informing them about their organization's DEI accomplishments and appreciating their efforts toward those achievements. This idea of celebrating DEI milestones is capable of motivating employees to keep doing their best in promoting DEI ideals among their peers and leaders.

A successful communication plan for conveying equity objectives and milestones centers on multiple essential elements:

- Clear and specific objectives: Ensuring that all stakeholders are aware of the organization's DEI goals requires clearly defining and articulating specific equity objectives. These goals should be SMART (specific, measurable, attainable, relevant, and time-bound) and should be in line with the organization's overarching strategic objectives.

Updates on DEI progress should be provided on a regular and consistent basis to keep stakeholders informed and involved. Maintaining uniformity in the structure and modes of communication guarantees that updates are easily discernible and obtainable.

- Engaging content and storytelling: DEI initiatives become more relatable and powerful when personal testimonies and stories are shared, humanizing them. Charts, infographics, and movies are examples of visual aids that make data and milestones easier to comprehend and visually appealing.

Chapter **10**

Significance of Diversity, Equity, and Inclusion: A Final Overview

This chapter considers, in detail, the practical benefits of implementing full-scale DEI policies at organizations. Some of the benefits include but are not limited to increased creativity and innovation, high employee morale, and the establishment of a working environment based on transparency, mutual respect, and trust. This chapter also delves into how well-executed DEI initiatives can help employees retain their existing jobs, prepare them for future opportunities, and enhance their skills for professional development, as an individual or a team. Each section combines research-based insights and best practices for organizations that aspire to jumpstart a new DEI initiative or refine their existing DEI practices.

Key learning objectives should include the reader's understanding of the following:

- Enhancing creativity and innovation across internal and external stakeholders

- Commencing a dei performance management team to elevate morale and reduce internal attrition

- Learning the steps in nurturing an environment of transparency and confidence

- Facilitating employee retention

- Encouraging employee empowerment for future advancement

10.1 Enhance Creativity and Innovation Across Internal and External Stakeholders

When organizations fully incorporate DEI principles into their cultures, such a confident move can lead to an unprecedented level of innovation and creativity within their systems. Diverse teams bring unique perspectives, experiences, and ideas that can inspire new solutions and approaches. This is an attempt to investigate how DEI fosters creativity and innovation among internal and external stakeholders, resulting in sustained competitive advantage and growth.

10.1.1 Internal stakeholders: Diverse teams

What makes diversity, equity, and inclusion (DEI) programs succeed in most companies are the internal stakeholders (mostly diverse employees) who are cooperatively working together on various aspects of their organization's DEI policies.

Here is how diverse teams are holding up their organization's DEI expectations:

- **A broad range of perspectives**: Diverse teams consist of people from various backgrounds, cultures, and experiences, resulting in a broader range of perspectives. This diversity encourages creative problem-solving because team members approach challenges from various perspectives.

- **Improved decision-making**: Research indicates that diverse teams make better decisions. Cloverpop found that diverse teams make decisions 60% faster than non-diverse teams and 87% better. This is because diversity reduces the possibility of groupthink and promotes critical evaluation of various ideas.

- **Innovation through collaboration**: Diverse teams are more inclined to collaborate effectively, resulting in the exchange of ideas and the development of innovative solutions. Collaboration between team members with diverse skill sets and perspectives can result in unique and innovative products and services.

10.1.2 Inclusive leadership

As already explained in Chapter 9, inclusive leadership is one of the major prerequisites for smoothly promoting DEI principles in any organization. Some of the additional advantages of inclusive leadership are highlighted below:

- **Creating an inclusive work environment**: Inclusive leaders create a supporting environment that recognizes valuable contributions from employees, irrespective of their cultural backgrounds and gender. Through this approach, they encourage the free exchange of creative ideas among diverse teams and urge employees to become critical thinkers.

- **Leveraging diverse strengths**: Inclusive leaders understand that everyone on their teams is unique and brings exceptional talent to the table. By taking advantage of a diverse team's talent pool, inclusive leaders can always rely on their diverse team members' skills to quickly get the job done. Such leaders also understand that showing appreciation and motivating employees can surely bring out the best in them.

- **Encouraging psychological safety**: Inclusive leaders understand that employees require some form of psychological safety before they can communicate their experiences and feelings openly without facing avoidable backlash from colleagues and superiors. By encouraging psychological safety at their workplaces, inclusive leaders give room for creative and transparent interactions among their employees.

10.1.3 External stakeholders: Customer insights

Customers are external motivators or stakeholders that hold organizations accountable for their DEI policies. Organizations that welcome employees from various cultural backgrounds and demographics tend to attract different customers from various demographics, too. As a matter of fact, organizations do flaunt their DEI rankings and achievements so as to attract customers from across many backgrounds and stay in business.

- **Understanding diverse markets:** Most organizations understand that employees from diverse backgrounds are better equipped and capable of handling customers from various demographics, most especially customers from their own cultures. This is true because they understand the customers' preferences, customs, and norms. Organizations that aspire to reach a wide variety of customers in diverse markets must create an environment that is attractive to diverse employees.

- **Improved customer engagement:** When diverse customers are well engaged and served, they will become loyal to the organizations giving them great customer experience. Organizations that have diverse employees possessing various skills and competencies are able to craft marketing strategies that will resonate with their target audiences. This can surprisingly lead to an increase in market share and customer loyalty.

10.1.4 Collaborations and partnerships

The main reason DEI-focused organizations form an alliance is to exchange vital ideas and best practices with one another.

- **Diverse networks:** DEI-focused organizations are often excited to join the networks of other companies whose operations are guarded by DEI ideas. Some of the benefits from this alliance include obtaining the latest ideas or solutions about diversity, equity, and inclusion, and collaborating on community development projects.

- **Innovation through external collaboration:** Innovation can be sparked by working with a variety of external stakeholders, including partners, suppliers, and community organizations. These partnerships may result in the co-creation of goods and services that cater to a broader spectrum of customers' needs.

10.2 Commencing a DEI Performance Management Team to Elevate Morale and Reduce Internal Attrition

It is a fact that many organizations adopt DEI principles for two, closely related reasons: To boost their employees' morale and to reduce their internal attrition rates. This section looks into the processes that can go into setting up a DEI performance management team at any organization. Efforts are also made to explain clearly the functions of the DEI performance management team, which include but are not limited to holding their organizations accountable for their DEI ideals (like creating a culture convenient to all demographics) and making recommendations for continuous improvements in their DEI practices.

- **Formation of the team**

  The success of a DEI performance management team is largely dependent on its makeup. The team should be composed of individuals from diverse departments and demographic backgrounds to guarantee a thorough and inclusive approach. By bringing a variety of viewpoints to the discussion, this diverse representation ensures that DEI strategies are comprehensive and consider the needs of the entire workforce. To get diverse opinions or perspectives about an organization's DEI progress, it is important to draw representatives from all the departments within the organization, from leadership, human resources, and employee resource groups (ERGs). It is helpful to select DEI performance management team members who are passionate about protecting DEI principles and working with all stakeholders to create a comfortable working environment for all employees.

- **Roles and responsibilities**

  DEI officers: These officers should be responsible for managing the implementation of DEI programs and policies in accordance with their organization's core values and goals.

  Data analysts: The DEI data analysts will be in charge of the organization's data, analyzing its metrics in relation to employee satisfaction, attrition rates, and diversity demographics.

  HR specialists: They are experts in incorporating DEI techniques into the hiring, onboarding, and performance review procedures.

  Employee advocates: They act as a point of contact for the DEI team and the larger workforce, making sure that suggestions and grievances raised by staff members are taken into consideration.

- **Strategies for operations**

  The effectiveness of the DEI performance management team will be dependent on the nature of the goals it is setting, based on the organization's general vision. It is advisable for the DEI performance management team to have SMART (Specific, measurable, achievable, realistic, time-bound) objectives. For example, the team may be overseeing the plan to double the number of underrepresented demographics in the organization within 2-3 years or include more women in leadership positions.

Tracking DEI progress or the impacts of DEI programs is a good approach for determining the efficacy of DEI practices within an organization. Using the available metrics, the DEI team can monitor which aspects of their organization's DEI practices are successful, and which areas still require some improvements. Data analytics can reveal useful information from metrics about employee promotion rates, employee satisfaction levels, retention rates, and increases in the hiring and onboarding of diverse talent. Without conducting this kind of evaluation, it may be practically difficult for an organization to know precisely how its employees' experiences are influenced by their DEI training and other DEI projects they are exposed to.

Transparency is the vehicle that will drive every organization's DEI initiatives to success. This entails that the DEI performance management team should promote open and respectful communication among all employees and stakeholders. Avenues such as departmental town hall meetings, newsletters, intranet, and internal reports should be utilized to spread useful information among employees, foster a spirit of togetherness, and be adopted as part of the organization's feedback loop. If necessary, leaders should be trained in demonstrating full commitment towards DEI efforts despite their very busy schedules, and their DEI performance should be one of their assessments of leadership.

- **Impact on morale and attrition**

  When an inclusive work environment where all staff members are treated with respect and feel appreciated is being created, it increases employee engagement and job satisfaction. Employee motivation and productivity are higher when they believe that their company is truly committed to diversity, equity, and inclusion. When employees are encouraged and genuinely appreciated for their efforts, they will be quite excited about their jobs. Sponsoring employees to seminars, workshops, mentorship programs, cultural events, and professional development programs can incredibly boost their morale. To strategically address the issue of employee retention, organizations need to first of all identify factors contributing to employee churn.

  Many employees have chosen to change jobs or left companies that they love owing to some issues that were not internally resolved by applying DEI principles. These may include but are not restricted to discrimination and microaggressions, lack of equal access to opportunities for professional development or career development, and demanding working schedules. To keep their hardworking employees, organizations need to take some deliberate steps to address the causes of employee attrition by providing flexible working schedules, creating equal chances for employees to grow, offering mental support, and promoting work-life balance.

10.3 Steps in Nurturing an Environment of Transparency and Confidence

An environment of trust is built on absolute transparency, and leaders should nurture confidence in their employees by being trustworthy, real, and dependable. DEI offers the management team a chance to win their subordinates' trust by demonstrating fairness and a welcoming attitude. When employees are recognized, respected, and supported by their leaders, they tend to perform at their best.

10.3.1 Steps to achieve transparency

Highlighted below are some strategic steps that should be taken before transparency can become the norm or status quo in an organization:

- **Open communication**

  A Harvard Business Review study revealed that transparency fosters trust and cooperation among team members (Groysberg & Slind, 2012). Every organization where open and respectful communication is promoted often has employees who are usually motivated to speak frankly about their DEI experiences, and who are willing to offer constructive criticisms of their organization's existing DEI practices so as to make a case for its improvement. Through the hosting of regular town hall meetings, interdepartmental discussion groups, Q&A sessions, and open-door policies, employees can feel comfortable to share their true DEI experiences with their colleagues and/ or superiors without worrying about any backlash.

- **Regular reporting**

  It is one of the best practices for organizations to release
  their monthly, quarterly, or yearly DEI reports outlining
  their achievements and challenges in promoting a
  culture of diversity, equity, and inclusion among their
  employees. IBM, a company well-known for its strong
  diversity stance, releases its diversity report annually and
  ensures that all its employees have access to the report.
  The report informs IBM employees of the company's
  DEI accomplishments, the interpretation of its DEI
  metrics, and the revelation about the progress of its DEI
  initiatives.

- **Making inclusive decisions**

  It is not enough to have great DEI policies in place,
  efforts must be deployed towards making actual
  inclusive decisions that will benefit all employees,
  irrespective of their cultural or demographic orientations.
  By engaging staff members in DEI activities and
  decision-making, that sense of belonging or ownership
  can go a long way to encouraging employees to embrace
  their organization's DEI initiatives wholeheartedly. To
  ensure that everyone's voice is heard, it is advisable
  to include virtually a representative from each
  demographic or department in the advisory council or
  decision-making committee.

- **Building confidence**

  In an organization, confidence arises from a culture that
  makes workers feel safe, appreciated, and in control. Such
  confidence-building calls for purposeful policies and
  actions:

Trust-building activities

Participating in trust-building exercises can improve the bonds between team members and between workers and management. A great DEI foundation can be established through community-building efforts, such as encouraging employees to participate in team-building activities, seminars, workshops, and conflict-resolution training. Being receptive to and respectful of others' viewpoints and ideas can build a formidable trust among people working together.

Dedicated leadership

Leaders who are truly committed to DEI ideals are often open and proud of their achievements in that regard. Their subordinates can also see that they embody DEI principles as revealed in their inclusive actions, decisions, and choices. Leaders who are dedicated to diversity and inclusivity are adept at quickly resolving issues arising from poorly executed DEI initiatives, such as discrimination, bias, and mistreatment. When their leaders are dedicated to DEI principles, employees will trust and collaborate with them in order to achieve success in their organization's DEI programs.

10.3.2 Long-term strategies

It is important for organizations to understand that maintaining transparency and trust among its employees demands a long-term commitment, and it requires some of the strategies explained below:

- **Policy development**

  DEI initiatives won't be effective without being backed by the appropriate policies. And when policies are well implemented, they can give rise to long-term openness and transparency within an organization. This entails that there should be well-defined procedures for reviewing employees' performance, listening to their complaints, resolving whatever problems they may be facing, and policies to eliminate discrimination and biases. It is equally important that such policies must be periodically updated so that they can be efficacious and applicable to the current scenarios.

- **Continuous improvement**

  It is imperative that organizations build into their systems and operations a culture of continuous improvement. Efforts must be deployed towards evaluating the DEI initiative every day, requesting useful contributions from employees, and carrying out any required modifications. As employees evolve, so do their professional aspirations; therefore, organizations should respond smartly to the dynamic changes their employees go through so as to maintain their DEI plans for a long time.

10.4 Facilitating Employee Retention

Every organization needs employees to run their day-to-day operations. This is why the issue of employee retention is an essential aspect of an organization's routine business activities. When fully implemented, DEI can be instrumental in increasing the employee retention rates for most organizations. It is a fact that employees thrive in an environment where they are respected, catered for, and motivated. It is fair to say that a good DEI policy can help a company attract and retain a diverse and great talent pool.

Talent retention demands an inclusive working environment for several reasons. Some of these are:

- **Increased job satisfaction**

  Higher job satisfaction rates have been directly linked to organizations with effective DEI programs. When workers are welcomed, included, appreciated, and respected, they tend to be happy and choose to remain working for the same organization for a long time.

- **Enhanced engagement**

  When DEI principles are fully implemented and employees feel included in the day-to-day affairs of their company, they will naturally feel obliged to contribute more and creatively to the activities going on there. This enhanced engagement can lead to higher productivity, better employee-to-employee relationships, and sustained employee-to-employer loyalty.

- **Decreased turnover**

  Very few employees will contemplate quitting an organization that has effective DEI policies in place, where biases, discrimination, and other unfavorable working conditions have been eliminated. This automatically leads to a decreased turnover.

- **Professional growth**

  DEI-focused organizations give all employees equal opportunities to grow professionally by streamlining their access to the organization's resources, aids, and programs.

10.4.1 Advantages of high retention rates for businesses

Organizations stand to gain a lot from retaining a great and creative talent pool in their folds, and highlighted below are some of the advantages of high retention rates for businesses:

- **Cost savings**: When employees are quitting not from an organization, there is no need to advertise a new position, hire, train, and onboard new hires. Organizations can save some direct and indirect recruiting expenses on the occasion of a high retention rate.

- **Enhanced productivity**: A high retention rate means that well-experienced and seasoned employees continue to work for an organization. Because they are already used to the day-to-day operational procedures and corporate culture, seasoned employees can produce more.

- **Increased morale**: A stable workforce is something that every organization expects to achieve. There are many benefits attached to having one's employees stay in the saddle for a long time. It means employees have already become accustomed to working together as a cohesive team, and they are usually excited to do their assigned duties. Having driven workers with high morale can help companies achieve their business goals within a set deadline.

- **Improved customer relationships**: The longer an employee stays in a company, the more experienced they become at serving their employers' customers.

A high turnover is not good for an organization that wants to accomplish great customer satisfaction, because every new hire has to be trained in how to handle customer service, and it may take a long time before they can master that.

- **Enhanced employer brand**: Organizations with exceptionally high retention rates often attract the best, suitably qualified talent. When people look for a lifetime job, they prefer companies with good reputations for taking good care of their employees or those with great DEI policies.

10.4.2 DEI retention strategies

The good news is that organizations can systematically increase their retention rates by adopting all or some of the practices described below:

- **Developing inclusive policies**: It is not enough for organizations to have excellent DEI policies, they must actually be incorporated into every activity conducted at the organizations' workplaces. One thing employees admire is that they are constantly included in their companies' daily operations, and decision-making process, and in accessing all tools and resources for professional growth. Any organization that includes its employees in its affairs and gives them the chance to voice their opinions when necessary will succeed in keeping such employees.

- **Providing DEI training**: Employees appreciate organizations that carry out regular DEI training for their employees, through which they will be taught how to avoid any actions that could undermine their colleagues' identity, integrity, and humanity. The most appropriate approach for removing biases and discrimination is to constantly remind people that such negative behavior is not acceptable within that corporate culture. And any employee that disrespects that rule should be recommended for certain punishment.

- **Encouraging employee resource groups (ERGs)**: It is believed that when organizations throw their full support behind the establishment of employee resource groups (ERGs) within their structures, they give their employees the assurance that they are an active part of the communities within those organizations. An ERG is a good place where employees freely meet, discuss, interact, seek support, and exchange ideas and opinions about their working experiences and the impacts of DEI policies on their satisfaction as employees.

- **Ensuring fair career development**: When given an equal chance to grow professionally, employees tend to appreciate such organizations by choosing to continue working for them. Some of the career development resources that should be accessible to all include but are not limited to mentorship programs, leadership courses, and seminars/workshops that can advance their career trajectories.

- **Encouraging work-life balance**: The modern-day employees appreciate employers that encourage a work-life balance. Some programs such as wellness initiatives, parental leave, and flexible work schedules can motivate workers to stay put in an organization.

10.5 Encouraging Employee Empowerment for Future Advancement

Employees invest their emotions and physical energy in companies that they admire and are happy to work for. Now, it is their employers' responsibility to sustain that motivation and impetus for as long as the employees work for them. This calls for empowering the employees for future performance. This section critically looks into what organizations can do to encourage their employees to perform at their best long-term.

10.5.1 Components of employee engagement

The concept of employee engagement is a complex one because it involves influencing human psychology in one way or the other. Here are some of the essential steps organizations can take to increase their employee engagement:

- **Emotional commitment**

  Employees will hold nothing back from companies they are emotionally connected to. This entails that they will consistently work so hard toward helping their employers achieve their organizational objectives or goals. In this case, organizations need to take good care of their employees and boost their morale to the extent that they will be willing to do their best for them.

- **Rational commitment**

  By knowing their place in a company, employees understand that it is just rational for them to carry out their assigned functions for their employer. However, organizations can encourage deliberate and purposeful commitment by creating an inclusive working environment for all their employees. Even though workers understand that it is their duty to do the jobs they are paid for, if they are exposed to discrimination and biases there, it may affect the quality of their work.

- **Behavioral engagement**

  DEI-focused organizations have a way of encouraging their employees to be proactively engaged with their work. By making them feel recognized, valued, and included in routine corporate affairs, companies can increase their employees 'level of commitment. Workers who are behaviorally engaged with their employers' goals take the initiative to carry out their assigned duties, work cooperatively with their colleagues, and constantly improve on their overall contributions at work.

10.5.2 Strategies for encouraging employee empowerment

These are some time-tested strategies for encouraging employee empowerment:

- **Providing autonomy:** Giving employees the power to make their own decisions while on the job is referred to as employee autonomy. Putting undue pressure on workers, maybe by the managers or supervisors, can cause them to be confused about their responsibilities. The most sensible approach to empowering employees is to let them decide for themselves.

- **Providing professional development**: Organizations that invest in their employees' continued education and training are serious about their professional development. By acquiring new ideas and techniques from various industry-related conferences, workshops, seminars, and educational courses, employees can systematically improve the quality of their work and help their organizations attain their corporate goals.

- **Establishing clear career pathways**: Employees are usually empowered to do more for companies that have clear career pathways for them to grow professionally. Knowing fully that after working for a company for 20-30 years they can be promoted to a senior position, employees will be emotionally and behaviorally connected to that company.

- **Creating a supportive environment**: Supportive leaders understand that they need to create an inclusive environment for all their employees. This is an important way to empower workers. More importantly, giving employees the much-needed psychological safety often encourages them to open up about their real experiences while working with other people at their company. They will be able to take the calculated risks of even challenging some of their employers' policies to ensure that everyone is being treated fairly.

- **Acknowledging and honoring contributions**: An organization that can greatly empower its employees through motivation; can be accomplished by simply acknowledging and honoring their wonderful contributions to the growth of the organization. Acknowledgments can also be in the form of giving them financial incentives such as prizes, verbal recognition, a salary raise, and promotions, irrespective of their cultural backgrounds.

Notes

Made in the USA
Columbia, SC
18 February 2025

54028931R00115